# The BIG TENNESSEE Reproducible Activity Book!

BY CAROLE MARSH

This activity book has material that correlates with Tennessee Social Studies Framework.

At every opportunity, we have tried to relate information to the History and Social Science, English, Science, Math, Civics, Economics, and Computer Technology Tennessee directives.

For additional information, go to our websites:
**www.tennesseeexperience.com** or **www.gallopade.com**.

Correlates with Tennessee's SSF Social Studies Framework™

Published by
GALLOPADE INTERNATIONAL™
800-536-2GET
www.gallopade.com

Reading Research Reinforcement Reference

Gallopade is proud to be a member or supporter of these educational organizations and associations:

NSSEA ASCD ABA AMERICAN BOOKSELLERS ASSOCIATION APPL SUPPORTER NCSS

# A Word From The Author

Tennessee is a very special state. Almost everything about Tennessee is interesting and fun! It has a remarkable history that helped create the great nation of America. Tennessee enjoys an amazing geography of incredible beauty and fascination. The state's people are unique and have accomplished many great things.

This Activity Book is chock-full of activities to entice you to learn more about Tennessee. While completing puzzles, coloring activities, word codes, and other fun-to-do activities, you'll learn about your state's history, geography, people, places, animals, legends, and more.

Whether you're sitting in a classroom, stuck inside on a rainy day, or—better yet—sitting in the back seat of a car touring the wonderful state of Tennessee, my hope is that you have as much fun using this Activity Book as I did writing it.

Enjoy your Tennessee Experience—it's the trip of a lifetime!!

Carole Marsh

# The Tennessee Experience Series

**The BIG Tennessee Wall Timeline**

**Tennessee Student Reference Timeline**

**My First Pocket Guide to Tennessee!**

**The Tennessee Coloring Book!**

**My First Book About Tennessee!**

**Tennessee Jeopardy:**
**Answers and Questions About Our State**

**Tennessee "Jography!":**
**A Fun Run Through Our State**

**The Tennessee Experience! Sticker Pack**

**The Tennessee Experience! Poster/Map**

**Discover Tennessee CD-ROM**

**Tennessee "HISTORY" Bingo Game**

**Tennessee "GEOGRAPHY" Bingo Game**

**Tennessee "BIOGRAPHY" Bingo Game**

Color Me!
Tennessee
BROWN
Brown like the graceful Tennessee Walking Horse.
Brown
BLUE
Blue like the raging Mississippi River.
Blue
YELLOW
Yellow like the colorful honeybee, firefly, and zebra swallowtail butterfly, all state symbols.
Yellow
RED
Red like the bright and blazing state flag.
Red
BLACK
Black like the ringed tail and mask on a raccoon, the state wild animal.
Black
PURPLE
Purple like the majestic Great Smoky Mountain peaks.
Purple
GREEN
Green like the peaceful Cherokee National Forest.
Green
ORANGE
Orange like the spirited Tennessee Volunteers sports teams!
Orange

# Geographic Tools

**Beside each geographic need listed, put the initials of the tool that can best help you!**

(CR) Compass Rose
(M) Map
(K) Map key/legend
(LL) Longitude and Latitude
(G) Grid

1. _____ I need to find the geographic location of Germany.
2. _____ I need to learn where an airport is located near Maryville.
3. _____ I need to find which way is North.
4. _____ I need to chart a route from Tennessee to California.
5. _____ I need to find a small town on a map.

**Match the items on the left with the items on the right.**

1. Grid system
2. Compass rose
3. Longitude and latitude
4. Two of Tennessee's borders
5. Symbols on a map

A. Map key or legend
B. Georgia and Kentucky
C. A system of letters and numbers
D. Imaginary lines around the earth
E. Shows N, S, E, and W

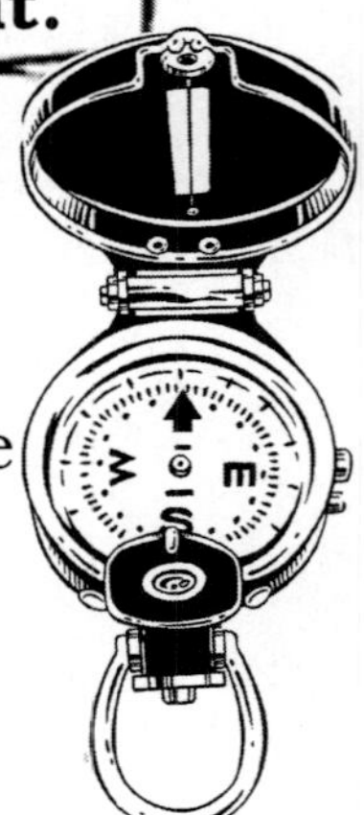


**ANSWERS:** 1-LL; 2-K; 3-CR; 4-M; 5-G; 1-C; 2-E; 3-D; 4-B; 5-A

# Tennessee's State Horse—Walking Tall!

The magnificent Tennessee Walking Horse is bred near Nashville. Tennessee Walkers have a long, graceful gait (stride) that's unique to this breed of saddle horse. They are bred to comfortably carry their riders for a long period of time. Tennessee Walkers also have a gentle disposition.

The Tennessee Walking Horse became a recognized breed in 1935. Famous Tennessee Walkers include F Allen One and Strolling Jim.

For 10 days each summer, folks get together in Shelbyville for "the Celebration." It's a famous festival and competition that's officially called the Tennessee Walking Horse National Celebration.

**Use the facts you've learned about Tennessee's state horse to answer these questions.**

1. Where are Tennessee Walking Horses bred?

   ______________________________________________

2. Tennessee Walkers have a _ _ _ _ that's special. It's a long stride that's comfortable for their riders over a long period of time.

3. True or False: Tennessee Walkers have a gentle disposition.

   ______________________________________________

4. When did Tennessee Walkers become a recognized breed?

   ______________________________________________

5. Name one famous Tennessee Walker.

   ______________________________________________

**ANSWERS:** 1-near Nashville; 2-gait; 3-True; 4-1935; 5-F Allen One or Strolling Jim

# Tennessee Government

Tennessee's state government, just like our national government, is made up of three branches. Each branch has a certain job to do. Each branch also has some power over the other branches. We call this system checks and balances. The three branches work together to make our government run smoothly.

| **Legislative Branch** | **Executive Branch** | **Judicial Branch** |
|---|---|---|
| Two Houses: Senate (33 members) House of Representatives (99 members) | A governor and department commissioners | Supreme Court: Chief Justice and four Associate Justices, intermediate appellate, general trial courts, and courts of limited jurisdiction |

**For each of these government officials, circle whether he or she is part of the EXECUTIVE, the LEGISLATIVE, or the JUDICIAL branch.**

| | | | | |
|---|---|---|---|---|
| 1. | Governor | EXECUTIVE | LEGISLATIVE | JUDICIAL |
| 2. | Intermediate Appellate Court Judge | EXECUTIVE | LEGISLATIVE | JUDICIAL |
| 3. | Commissioner of Tourism | EXECUTIVE | LEGISLATIVE | JUDICIAL |
| 4. | State Representative | EXECUTIVE | LEGISLATIVE | JUDICIAL |
| 5. | State Senator | EXECUTIVE | LEGISLATIVE | JUDICIAL |
| 6. | Supreme Court Justice | EXECUTIVE | LEGISLATIVE | JUDICIAL |
| 7. | Supreme Court Associate Justice | EXECUTIVE | LEGISLATIVE | JUDICIAL |
| 8. | Commissioner of Agriculture and Commerce | EXECUTIVE | LEGISLATIVE | JUDICIAL |
| 9. | Commissioner of Education | EXECUTIVE | LEGISLATIVE | JUDICIAL |
| 10. | General Trial Court Judge | EXECUTIVE | LEGISLATIVE | JUDICIAL |

**ANSWERS:** 1-Executive; 2-Judicial; 3-Executive; 4-Legislative; 5-Legislative; 6-Judicial; 7-Judicial; 8-Executive; 9-Executive; 10-Judicial

# All Around Tennessee! Bubblegram

Bubble up on your knowledge of Tennessee's bordering states.

**Fill in the bubblegram by using the clues below.**

1. A state to the northeast
2. A state to the northwest
3. A state to the south
4. A state to the north
5. A state to the east
6. A state to the southeast

1. (O) __ __ __ __ __ __ __
2. __ __ __ __ (O) __ __ __
3. __ (O) __ __ __ __ __
4. __ __ __ __ (O) __ __ __
5. (O) __ __ (O) __

   __ __ __ __ __ __ __ __
6. __ (O) __ (O) __ __ __

**Now unscramble the "bubble" letters to find out the mystery words!**

**Mystery Message:**

Tennessee's nickname is The __ __ __ __ __ __ __ e __ State

**ANSWERS:** 1-Virginia; 2-Missouri; 3-Alabama; 4-Kentucky; 5-North Carolina; 6-Georgia
**Mystery Message:** Volunteer

# Rhythmic Rebus!

**Use the rebus clues to name the titles of some Tennessee state songs.**

1. M +  +  + land + 10 + S + C =

“__ _________ ___________”

adopted in 1925; words by Nell Grayson Taylor; music by Roy Lamont Smith

2. W +  +  +  + 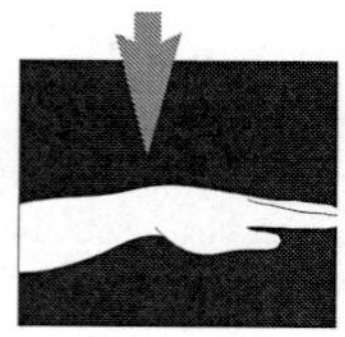 +  +  +  = “____ __'__ ____ ____ __ _________”

adopted in 1935; by Willa Waid Newman

3.  +  +  + ZZZ =

“_________ _____”

adopted in 1965; by Redd Stewart and Pee Wee King

4.  +  +  =

“_____ ___”

adopted in 1982; by Boudleaux and Felice Bryant

5. The +  + 

+ 10 + 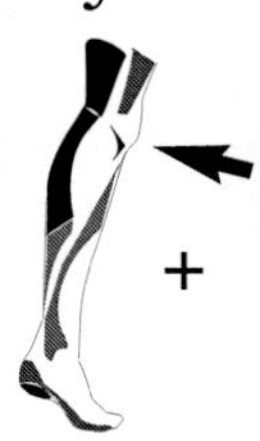 +  =

“___ _____ __ _________”

adopted in 1996; by Fred Congdon, Thomas Vaughn, and Carol Elliot

**ANSWERS:** 1-"My Homeland Tennessee"; 2-"When It's Iris Time in Tennessee"; 3-"Tennessee Waltz"; 4-"Rocky Top"; 5-"The Pride of Tennessee"

# Tennessee Wheel of Fortune, Native American Style!

The names of Tennessee's many Native American tribes contain enough consonants to play . . . Wheel of Fortune!

**See if you can figure out the Wheel of Fortune-style puzzles below! "Vanna" has given you some of the consonants in each word.**

C H _ _ _ K _ _

_ R _ _ _

_ H _ _ K _ _ _ W

S _ _ _ N _ _

Y _ _ _ _

**ANSWERS:** Cherokee; Creek; Chickasaw; Shawnee; Yuchi

# Rainbow, Pretty Rainbow

Spectacular rainbows often appear over Roan Mountain after a storm. Rainbows are formed when sunlight bends through raindrops. Big raindrops produce the brightest, most beautiful rainbows. You can see rainbows early or late on a rainy day when the sun is behind you.

**Color the rainbow in the order the colors are listed below, starting at the top of the rainbow. Then, in each band write down as many Tennessee-related words as you can think of that begin with the same first letter as that color!**

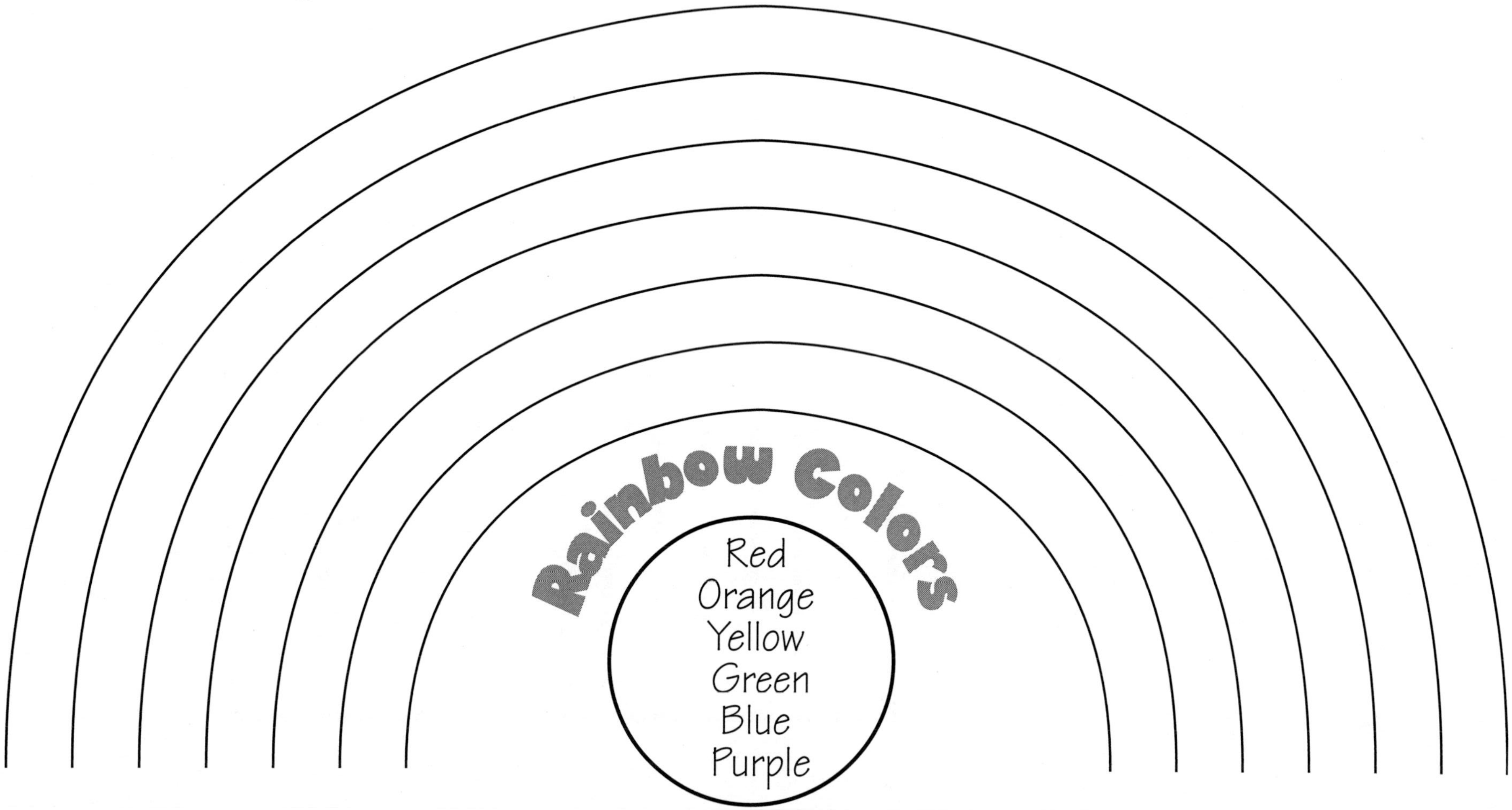

# In The Beginning... There Was A Settlement

During the 1540s, Spanish explorers passed through present-day Tennessee looking for gold. British explorers followed about a hundred years later. They were looking for treasures and new lands. French explorers canoed down the Mississippi River in 1682 and claimed the entire Mississippi River Valley for France. The French had come to stay. In 1714, a French trading post was built at French Lick, near present-day Nashville.

In the early 1700s, France, Spain, and Great Britain had claims on Tennessee. By 1754, Spain no longer claimed ownership, leaving the region of Tennessee to France and Great Britain.

**Help the French find their way to French Lick!**

Pioneers lived in small, isolated settlements. They built forts for protection.

# U.S. Time Zones

Would you believe that the contiguous United States is divided into four time zones? It is! Because of the rotation of the earth, the sun appears to travel from east to west. Whenever the sun is directly overhead, we call that time noon.

The state of Tennessee is divided into two time zones. Eastern Tennessee is in Eastern Standard Time (EST) and Western Tennessee is in Central Standard Time (CST). When it is noon in Memphis (CST), the sun has a long way to go before it is directly over San Francisco, California. When it is 12:00 p.m. (noon) in Knoxville (EST) it is 11:00 a.m. in Chicago, Illinois. There is a one-hour time difference between each zone!

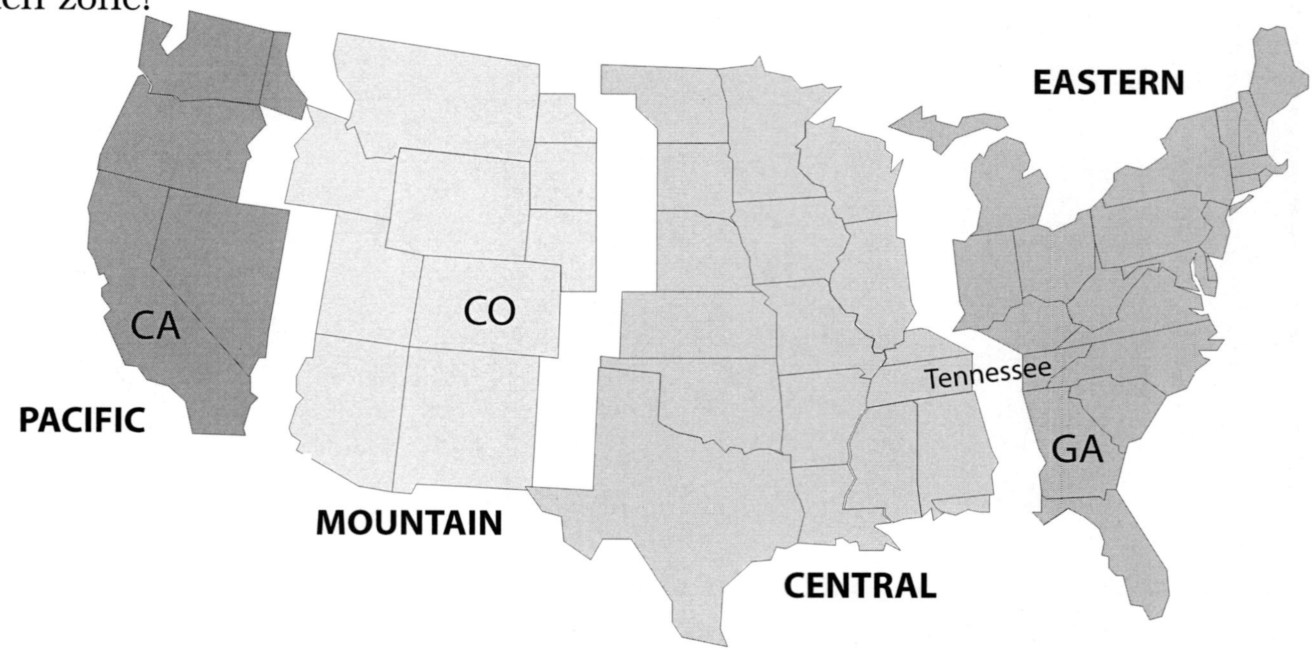


**Look at the time zones on the map below then answer the following questions:**

1. When it is 10:00 a.m. in Nashville, Tennessee, what time is it in California? ________ a.m.
2. When it is 3:30 p.m. in Atlanta, Georgia, what time is it in Oak Ridge, Tennessee? ________ p.m.
3. Tennessee is located in what two time zones? ________________________ and ________________________
4. In what time zone is Colorado located? ___________________
5. If it is 10:00 p.m. in Jackson, Tennessee, what time is it in Wyoming? _______ p.m.

**ANSWERS:** 1-8:00 a.m.; 2-3:30 p.m.; 3-Eastern Standard Time and Central Standard Time; 4-Mountain; 5-9:00 p.m.

# Sing Like a Tennessee Bird Word Jumble

**BIRD BANK**
blackbird
bobwhite quail
cardinal
crow
goldfinch
mockingbird
owl
robin
sparrow
woodpecker

**Arrange the jumbled letters in the proper order for the names of birds found in Tennessee.**

etihwbob liauq _ _ _ _ _ _ _ _ _ _ _ _ _ _

rowspar _ _ _ _ _ _ _

oodwkerpec _ _ _ _ _ _ _ _ _ _

low _ _ _

rowc _ _ _ _

binro _ _ _ _ _

birdingcomk _ _ _ _ _ _ _ _ _ _ _

lanidrca _ _ _ _ _ _ _ _

inchfdolg _ _ _ _ _ _ _ _ _

lcbrbakid _ _ _ _ _ _ _ _ _

**ANSWERS:** bobwhite quail; sparrow; woodpecker; owl; crow; robin; mockingbird; cardinal; goldfinch; blackbird

# Tennessee Schools Rule!

Tennessee has more than 70 public and private colleges and universities to help prepare students for a successful future! The University of Tennessee has campuses in different locations. You can become a "Vol" in several cities including Knoxville, Chattanooga, and Memphis.

**Complete the names of these Tennessee schools. Use the Word Bank to help you. Then use the answers to solve the code at the bottom.**

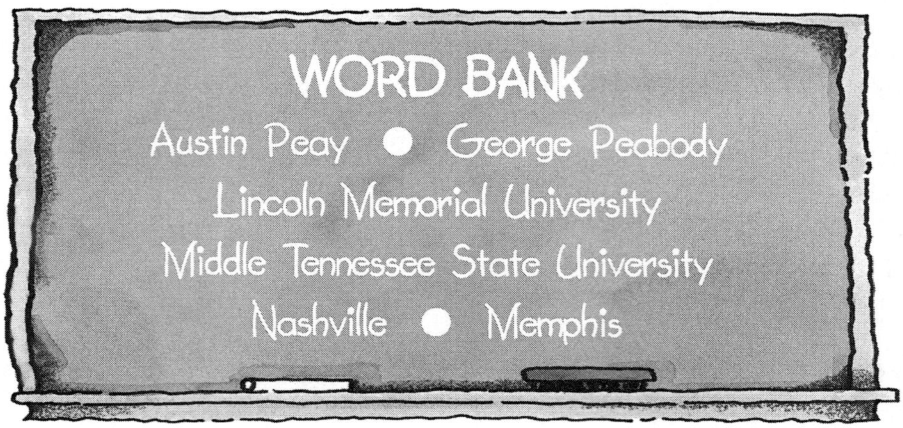


1. Vanderbilt University in Nashville includes ___ ___ ___ ___ ___ ___
   _3_ ___ ___ ___ ___ _1_ ___ College for Teachers
2. Fisk University in ___ ___ ___ ___ ___ _2_ ___ ___ ___
3. _4_ ___ ___ ___ _5_ ___ ___ ___ ___ ___ ___ ___ ___ ___ ___
   ___ ___ ___ ___ ___ ___ ___ ___ ___ ___ in Harrogate
4. ___ ___ ___ ___ ___ ___ ___ ___ ___ ___ ___ ___ ___ ___ ___ ___ ___ ___ ___ ___ ___
   ___ ___ ___ ___ ___ ___ ___ ___ ___ ___ in Murfreesboro
5. University of _6_ ___ ___ ___ ___ ___ ___
6. _7_ ___ ___ ___ ___ ___ ___ ___ ___ ___ State University in Clarksville

The coded message tells you what all college students want!

___ ___ ___ ___ ___ ___ ___
1 2 3 4 5 6 7.

**ANSWERS:** 1-George Peabody; 2-Nashville; 3-Lincoln Memorial University; 4-Middle Tennessee State University; 5-Memphis; 6-Austin Peay
**MESSAGE:** diploma

# Tennessee Topography is "Tops"!

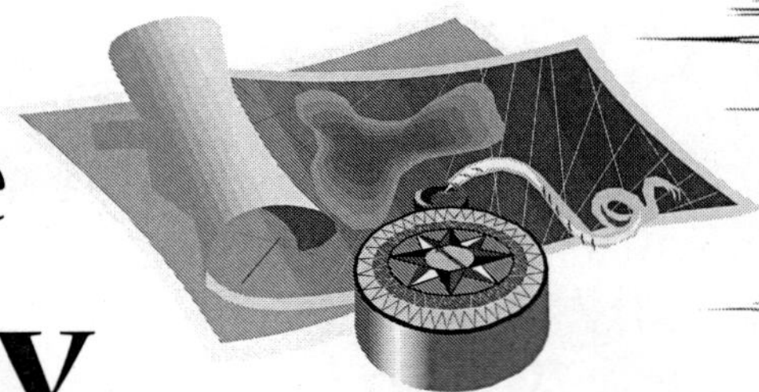

Tennessee's topography can be divided into East, Middle, and West. East Tennessee has mountains, ridges, coves, and valleys. Middle Tennessee has high hills and a basin with rich farmland. Nestled between the Tennessee River and the Mississippi River are the rolling hills and flatlands of West Tennessee.

When we learn about Tennessee's topography, we use special words to describe it. These words describe the things that make each part of the state interesting.

**Cross out every other letter below beginning with the first one to find out what each topographical term is!**

1. A G W O C R K G L E: a deep, narrow passage between mountains =

2. X B Z A E S E I T N: a large hollow, often filled with water =

3. Z V C A E L A L N E M Y: low land lying between hills or mountains =

4. B R E I Q D C G S E: long, narrow elevation of land =

5. P F E L B A A T P L C A L N Q D: expanse of land that does not vary in height above sea level =

6. T M Q O W U R N I T S A V I T N U S: chain or group of very high hills =

7. F H G I A L B L T S: ground higher than the land around it, but not as high as mountains =

8. P T A O Y P U O M G Q R T A O P V H K Y: the detailed mapping of the features on the surface of land =

**ANSWERS:** 1-gorge; 2-basin; 3-valley; 4-ridge; 5-flatland; 6-mountains; 7-hills; 8-topography

# Oh! Say Can You See... The Tennessee State Flag

Tennessee's current state flag was adopted in 1905. It features a geometric design of three white stars in a blue circle on a field of red. The stars represent three distinctly different regions, the Grand Divisions of the state—East, Middle, and West. The stars are eternally bound by an unending white band.

**Color the Tennessee flag.**

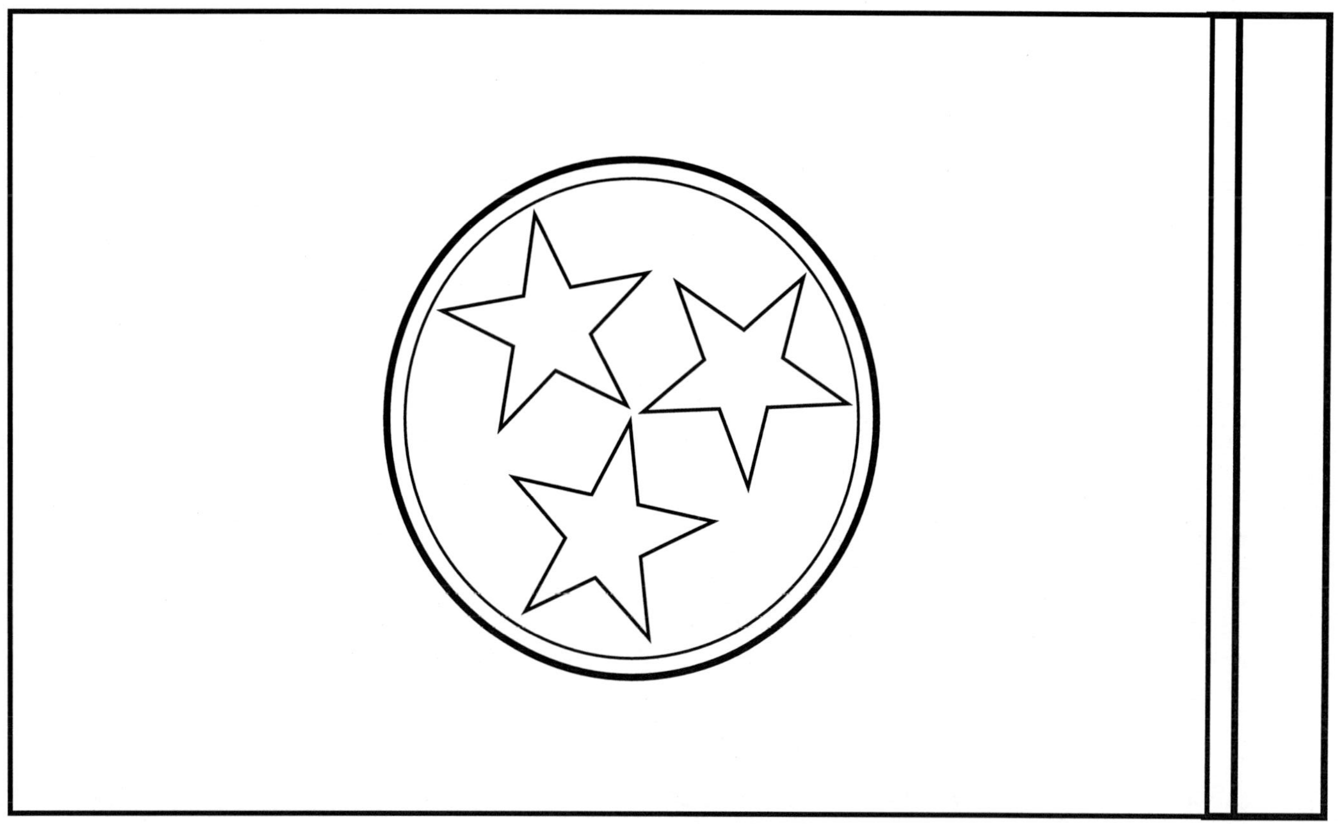

# Design Your Own Diamante About Tennessee!

A *diamante* is a cool diamond-shaped poem on any subject.

**You can write your very own diamante poem on Tennessee by following the simple line by line directions below. Give it a try!**

Line 1: Write the name of the state (one word).
Line 2: Write the names of two animals native to Tennessee (two words total).
Line 3: Write the names of three cities in Tennessee (three words total).
Line 4: Write the names of four of Tennessee's agricultural products (four words total).
Line 5: Write the names of three Tennessee birds (three words total).
Line 6: Write the names of Tennessee's state insects (two words total).
Line 7: Write the word that completes this sentence (one word total): Tennessee's nickname is the ____________________ State.

______________

______________ ______________

______________ ______________ ______________

______________ ______________ ______________ ______________

______________ ______________ ______________

______________ ______________

______________

# History Mystery Tour!

Tennessee is bursting at the seams with history! Here are just a few of the many historical sites that you might visit! Try your hand at locating them on the map! Draw the symbol for each site on the Tennessee map below.

**The Hermitage in Nashville**: The home of Andrew and Rachel Jackson. Andrew Jackson was the seventh U.S. president. The home and grounds are beautifully preserved.

**Shiloh National Military Park and Cemetery:** Located southeast of Savannah, this site was one of the bloodiest battles of the Civil War. For two days, Union and Confederate forces fought for their country and their lives—24,000 soldiers lost the fight and died.

**Beale Street Historic District**: Historic district in downtown Memphis where W.C. Handy wrote "Memphis Blues," "St. Louis Blues," and other classic, classy jazz tunes!

**Chucalissa Indian Village and Museum:** An archaeological project in Memphis. It's the site of a Native American village that dates back to AD 900. Several buildings have been reconstructed and Native Americans demonstrate traditional crafts.

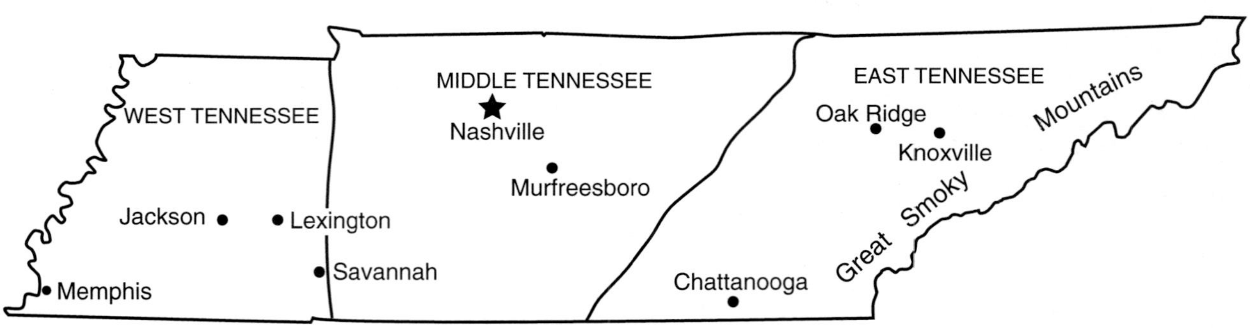

# What in the World?

A hemisphere is one-half of a sphere (globe) created by the prime meridian or equator. Every place in the world is in two hemispheres (Northern or Southern and Eastern or Western). The equator is an imaginary line that runs around the world from left to right and divides the globe into the Northern Hemisphere and the Southern Hemisphere. The prime meridian is an imaginary line that runs around the world from top to bottom and divides the globe into the Eastern Hemisphere and Western Hemisphere.

**Label the Northern and Southern Hemispheres.**

**Write E on the equator.**

**Is Tennessee in the NORTHERN or SOUTHERN Hemisphere? (circle one)**

**Color the map.**

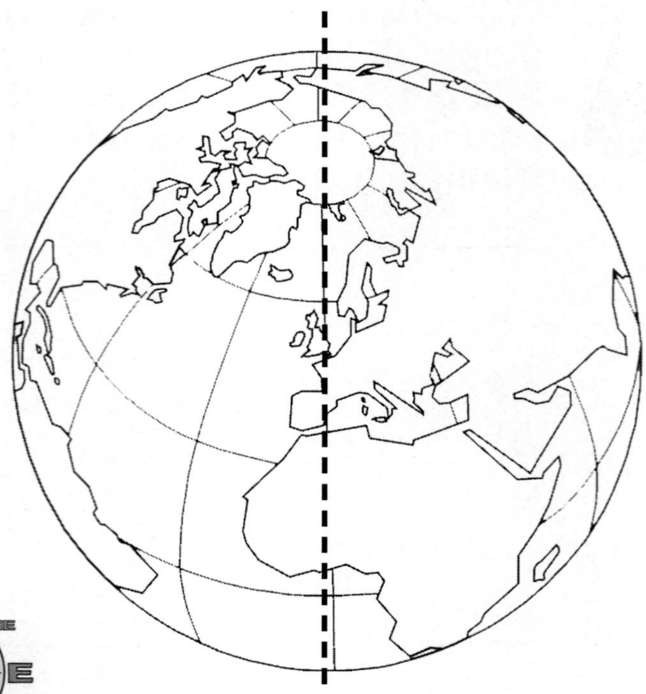

**Label the Eastern and Western Hemispheres.**

**Write PM on the prime meridian.**

**Is Tennessee in the EASTERN or WESTERN Hemisphere? (circle one)**

**Color the map.**

**ANSWERS:** Northern; Western

# Places to Go! Things to Do!

Tennessee has so many cool places to go and so many cool things to do! **Use the Word Bank to help you complete the sentences below and learn about some of the exciting Tennessee sites you can visit!**

1. Tennessee _ _ _ _ _ _ _ _, Chattanooga
2. _ _ _ _ _ _-_ _ _ _   _ _ _ _ _ _ Wilderness and Buzzard Point, Dayton
3. _ _ _ _ _ _ _ _ _ Zoo at Grassmere
4. Tennessee _ _ _ _ _ _ _ _   _ _ _ _ _ _ _ _   _ _ _ _ _ _, Paris
5. _ _ _ _ _ _   _ _ _ _ State Natural Area, Clarksville
6. Cheatham Wildlife Management Area, _ _ _ _ _ _ _   _ _ _ _
7. _ _ _   _ _ _ _ _ _ _   _ _ _ _ State Natural Area, Greenfield
8. Burgess Falls _ _ _ _ _   _ _ _ _ _ _ _   _ _ _ _, Cookeville

**WORD BANK**

| | |
|---|---|
| Aquarium | Laurel-Snow Pocket |
| Ashland City | Nashville |
| Big Cypress Tree | National Wildlife Refuge |
| Dunbar Cave | State Natural Area |

**ANSWERS:** 1-Aquarium; 2-Laurel-Snow Pocket; 3-Nashville; 4-National Wildlife Refuge; 5-Dunbar Cave; 6-Ashland City; 7-Big Cypress Tree; 8-State Natural Area

# Please Come to Tennessee!

You have a friend who lives in Georgia. She is thinking of moving to Tennessee because she wants to be a country music star, and Nashville is the **"Country Music Capital of the World."**

**Write her a letter describing Tennessee and some of the country music opportunities here.**

Nashville's rise to "Music City, USA" started back in 1925 when an insurance company started a radio station. WSM broadcast a program entitled "Barn Dance" that featured folk music from the Appalachian Mountains. The ballads of folk music blossomed into the songs of "country music" and in 1927, the show's name was changed to "The Grand Ole Opry." The Grand Ole Opry is the longest continuously running live radio program in the world! It's been broadcast every week since 1925. *Live from the Grand Ole Opry...!*

# A Time of Battles, Bravery, and Blood!

The Civil War was fought between the American states from 1861 to 1865. The argument was over states' rights to make their own decisions, including whether or not to own slaves. Southern states, with plantations and slaves, were on one side of this conflict. Northern states, which opposed slavery or had no need of it, were on the other side.

Some of the southern states began to secede (leave) the Union. They formed the Confederate States of America. Tennessee was the last southern state to secede and the first to be readmitted after the war ended.

**Take a crossword-puzzle tour of some of Tennessee's Civil War battle sites.**

Some Tennesseans fought for the North; some fought for the South!

Tennessee sent more soldiers into battle than any other state.

More Civil War battles were fought in the state of Tennessee than in all the states other than Virginia.

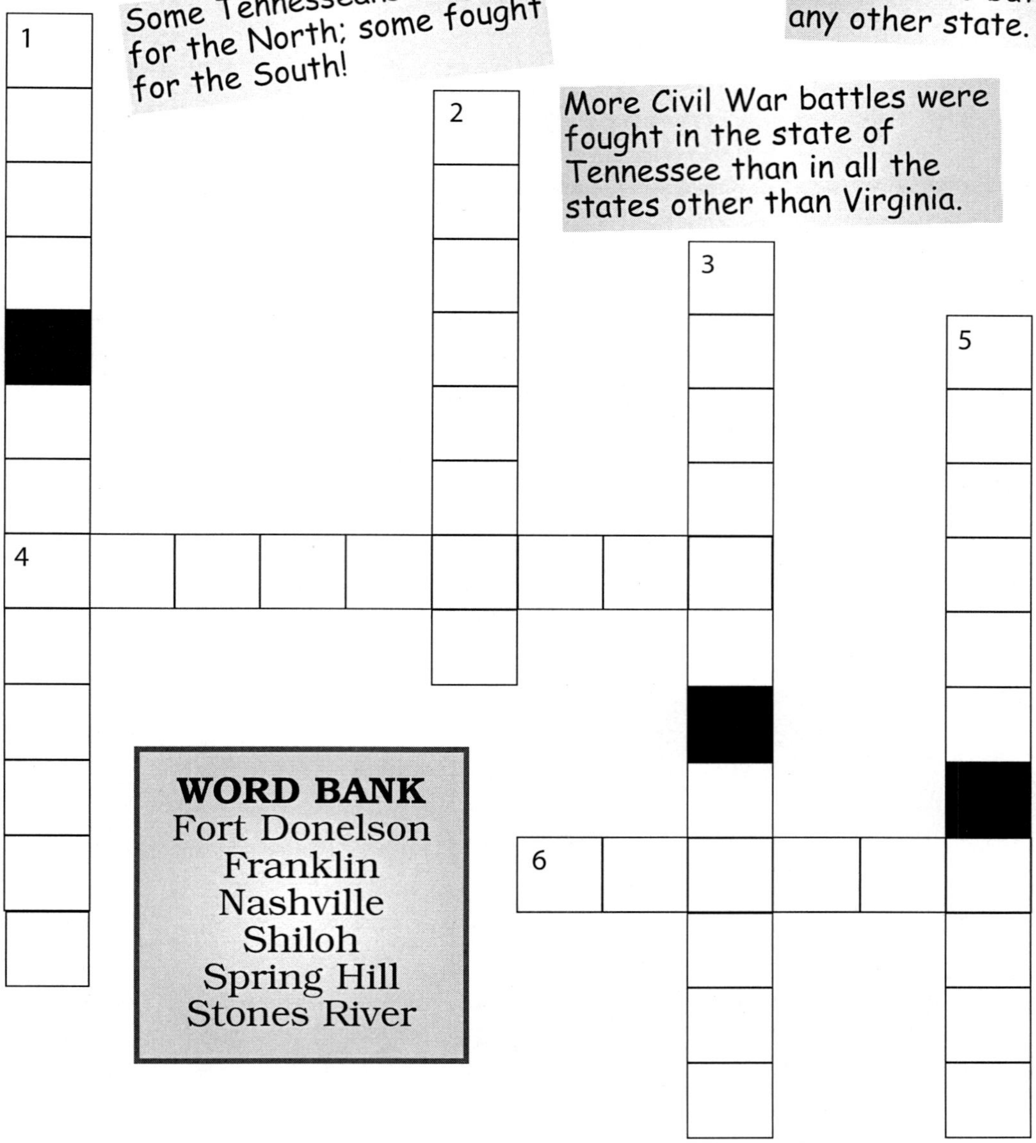


**WORD BANK**
Fort Donelson
Franklin
Nashville
Shiloh
Spring Hill
Stones River

**ANSWERS:** Across: 4-Nashville; 6-Shiloh; Down: 1-Fort Donelson; 2-Franklin; 3-Stones River; 5-Spring Hill

# Tennessee Rules!

**Use the code to complete the sentences.**

| A | B | C | D | E | F | G | H | I | J | K | L | M | N | O | P |
|---|---|---|---|---|---|---|---|---|---|---|---|---|---|---|---|
| **1** | **2** | **3** | **4** | **5** | **6** | **7** | **8** | **9** | **10** | **11** | **12** | **13** | **14** | **15** | **16** |

| Q | R | S | T | U | V | W | X | Y | Z |
|---|---|---|---|---|---|---|---|---|---|
| **17** | **18** | **19** | **20** | **21** | **22** | **23** | **24** | **25** | **26** |

1. State rules are called ___ ___ ___ ___.
   12 1 23 19

2. Laws are made in our state ___ ___ ___ ___ ___ ___ ___.
   3 1 16 9 20 15 12

3. The leader of our state is the ___ ___ ___ ___ ___ ___ ___ ___.
   7 15 22 5 18 14 15 18

4. We live in the state of ___ ___ ___ ___ ___ ___ ___ ___ ___.
   20 5 14 14 5 19 19 5 5

5. The capital of our state is ___ ___ ___ ___ ___ ___ ___ ___ ___.
   14 1 19 8 22 9 12 12 5

# T E N N E S S E E !

**ANSWERS:** 1-laws; 2-capitol; 3-governor; 4-Tennessee; 5-Nashville

# Buzzing Around Tennessee!

**Write the answers to the questions below. To get to the beehive, follow a path through the maze.**

1. Davy was born here: Davy _ _ _ _ _ _ _ _ Birthplace State Park, Limestone
2. Don't try to make a monkey out of me: _ _ _ _ _ _ _ _ _ _ _ Museum and Rhea County Courthouse, Dayton
3. That's hot, backbreaking work! _ _ _ _ _ _ _ _ _ _ _ _ _ _ _ Historic Site and Museum of Mining Artifacts
4. Frankly my dear, it's one of the most visited antebellum plantations in Tennessee. It's known as the Queen of Tennessee Plantations: _ _ _ _ _ _ _ _ _ _ _ _ _ _ _ _ _ _ _ _ in Nashville
5. Your loss, my gain! _ _ _ _ _ _ _ _ _ _ _ _ _ Plantation in Mt. Pleasant, built by George W. Polk on land won during a game of chance called "Rattle and Snap"
6. All Aboard! _ _ _ _ _ _ _ _ _ _ _ _ _ _ _ _ _ _ _ _
7. Wheeee! Let's ride again! _ _ _ _ _ _ _ _ _ in Pigeon Forge
8. A fright-filled visit to a frightful cave: _ _ _ _ _ _ _ _ _ _ _ _ _ _ in Adams
9. Up, Up, Up to the Tip Top: _ _ _ _ _ _ _ _ _ _ _ _ _ _ _ _ Incline Railway, Chattanooga
10. Wow! How did they do that? American Museum of _ _ _ _ _ _ _ _ _ _ _ _ _ _ _ _ _ _ _ in Oak Ridge

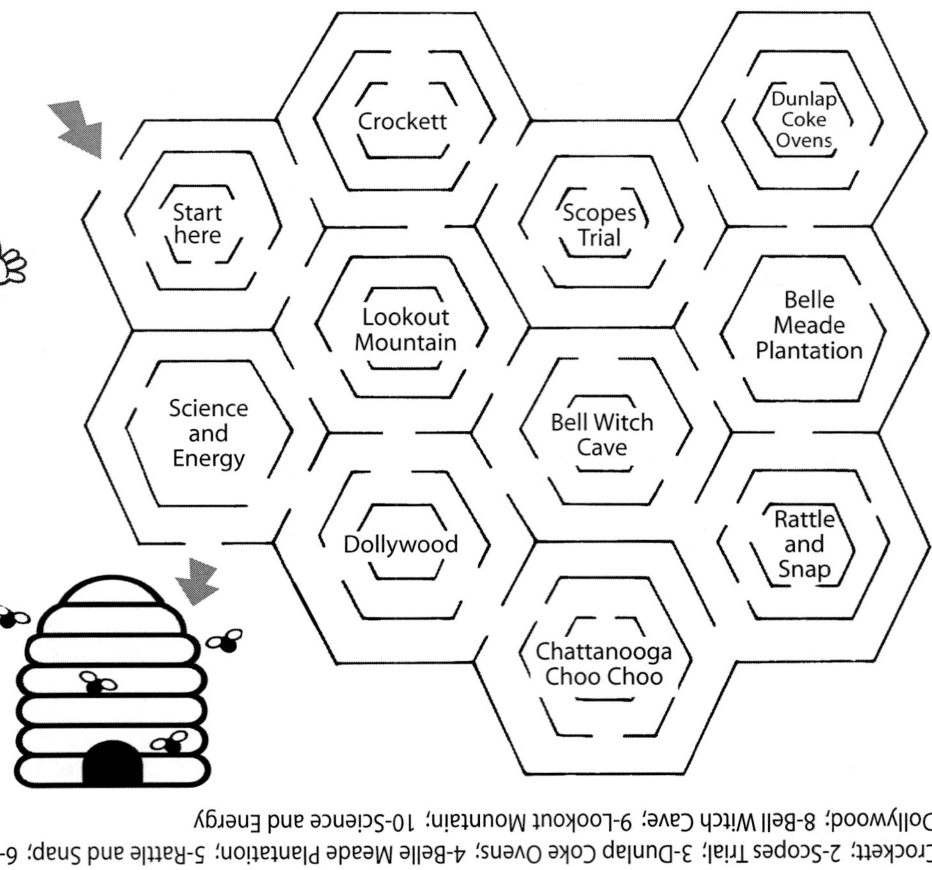


**ANSWERS:** 1-Crockett; 2-Scopes Trial; 3-Dunlap Coke Ovens; 4-Belle Meade Plantation; 5-Rattle and Snap; 6-Chattanooga Choo Choo; 7-Dollywood; 8-Bell Witch Cave; 9-Lookout Mountain; 10-Science and Energy

# Tennessee Through the Years!

**Many great things have happened in Tennessee throughout its history. Chronicle the following important Tennessee events by solving math problems to find out the years in which they happened.**

1. French establish trading post at French Lick.
   6÷6= 3+4= 4-3= 2x2=

2. Dr. Thomas Walker leads explorers through upper East Tennessee and discovers Cumberland Gap.
   7-6= 9-2= 8-3= 9-9=

3. Watauga Association adopts one of North America's first written documents of self-government.
   2-1= 8-1= 5+2= 9-7=

4. North Carolina gives Tennessee region to the United States.
   1+0= 6+1= 4x2= 6+3=

5. Andrew Jackson and Tennessee volunteers defeat British at the Battle of New Orleans.
   7-6= 7+1= 3-2= 2+3=

6. Civil War begins; Tennessee secedes.
   2-1= 4x2= 3x2= 8-7=

7. Civil War ends.
   2-1= 4x2= 3x2= 8-3=

8. Tennessee is readmitted to Union.
   1÷1= 5+3= 6x1= 9-3=

9. Nashville Metropolitan Board of Education settles 28-year dispute over school desegregation.
   3÷3= 6+3= 6+2= 9-6=

10. Tennessee celebrates 200th anniversary of the U.S. presidency by honoring state's three native sons who became president.
    (9-7)-1= (8+2)-1= (4x3)-4= (3x2)+3=

**BONUS:** Who are the three Tennessee natives who became president?

**ANSWERS:** 1-1714; 2-1750; 3-1772; 4-1789; 5-1815; 6-1861; 7-1865; 8-1866; 9-1983; 10-1989
**BONUS:** Andrew Jackson; James Polk; Andrew Johnson

# What Did We Do Before Money?

In early Tennessee, there were no banks. However, people still wanted to barter, trade, or otherwise "purchase" goods from each other. Wampum, made of shells, bone, or stones, was often swapped for goods. Indians, especially, used wampum for "money." In the barter system, people swapped goods or services.

Later, banks came into existence, and people began to use money to buy goods. However, they also still bartered when they had no money to spend.

The state of Tennessee's early economy was based on agricultural products and the iron produced in Middle Tennessee. After the Civil War, Tennessee's economy was in terrible shape. President Andrew Johnson introduced a policy of Reconstruction that started the country on the road to recovery.

**Place a star in the box below the systems used today.**

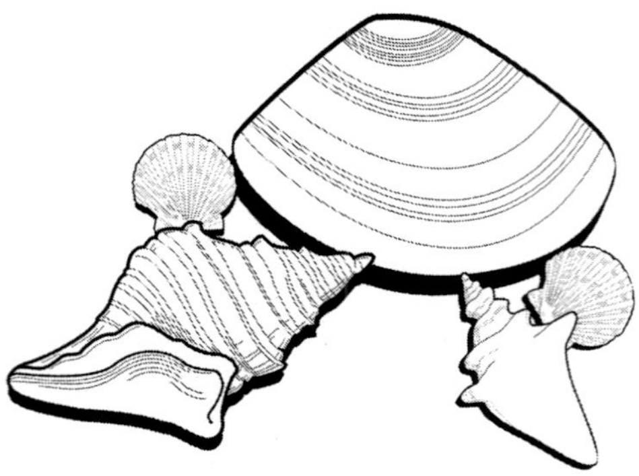

# Rhymin' Riddles

1. I am a southern state and my name starts with a "T"!
   I am that southern state and my name ends with an "E"!
   **What am I?** ____________________________

2. We came to this land from across the sea in search of furs;
   Charles Charleville was the first of our explorers.
   **Who are we?** ____________________________

3. I came to a new land with soldiers and guns and was quite bold!
   We wanted new land, Christian converts, and lots of gold!
   **Who am I?** ____________________________

4. Over the hills and through the woods I did go;
   For a path through the Appalachians settlers could know!
   **Who am I?** ____________________________

**ANSWERS:** 1-Tennessee; 2-French; 3-Hernando de Soto; 4-Dr. Thomas Walker

# Map Symbols

**Make up symbols for these names and draw them in the space provided on the right.**

| | |
|---|---|
| mountain | |
| river | |
| battlefield | |
| horse farm | |
| airport | |
| train | |
| capital | |
| mining | |
| state gem | |

# Tennessee Goodies!

**Match the name of each crop or product from Tennessee with the picture of that item.**

Nearly one half of Tennessee is farmland. Soybeans and tobacco are the most important crops and grow in East and Middle Tennessee. Cotton grows in West Tennessee.

strawberries

soybeans

corn

eggs

dairy products

honey

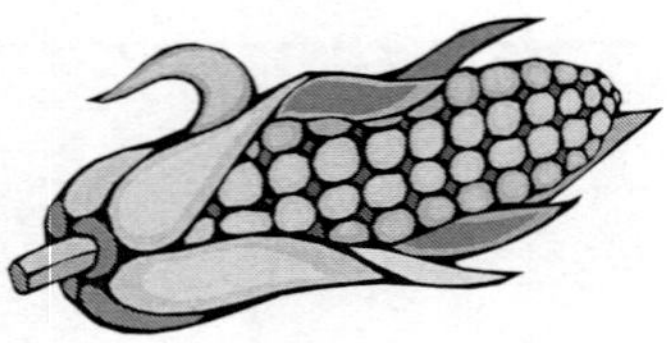

Livestock produces more than half of the state's income from agriculture. Cattle, hogs, and sheep are raised in Middle Tennessee where the grazing land is good for the livestock.

The famous Tennessee Walking Horse is also raised in Middle Tennessee near Nashville.

# Historical Tennessee Women Wonders!

**Tennessee has been the home of many brave and influential women. See if you can match these women with their accomplishments.**

1. Sue Shelton White
2. Dr. Rhea Seddon
3. Pat Head Summitt
4. Dr. Emma Rochelle Wheeler
5. Dr. Dorothy Brown
6. Kate Augusta Carl
7. Camille McGee Kelley
8. Emma Bell Miles
9. Grace Moore
10. Oprah Winfrey

A. Established Walden Hospital for African Americans in Chattanooga; founded a nursing school; worked to improve medical treatment for African Americans

B. Attorney, writer, suffragist, political activist, member of Tennessee Equal Suffrage Association and National Woman's Party

C. First woman judge in the South; second woman judge in the nation

D. Painter, educator; best known for portrait of last Empress Dowager of China

E. One of first six women in space; traveled to space for seven days aboard the space shuttle *Discovery*

F. Surgeon, educator, legislator; first African American woman to practice surgery in the South; first African American woman elected to General Assembly

G. Successful coach of National Champion Lady Vols; elected to Basketball Hall of Fame in 2000

H. Actress; talk-show hostess; news reporter; first Miss Black Tennessee

I. Painter, author, teacher; wrote eloquently about life in the mountains of Tennessee

J. Opera singer; known as "the Tennessee Nightingale"; sang in New York on Broadway and at the Metropolitan Opera

**ANSWERS:** 1-B; 2-E; 3-G; 4-A; 5-F; 6-D; 7-C; 8-I; 9-J; 10-H

# Producers and Consumers

Producers (sellers) make goods or provide services. Ralph, a fourth grade student in Memphis, is a consumer because he wants to buy a new wheel for his bicycle. Other products and services from Tennessee that consumers can buy include clothing, the writing of songs, electronic equipment, furniture, and Appalachian arts and crafts.

The Appalachian Mountains are famous for celebrated crafts and craftspeople. Handmade quilts, pottery, baskets, furniture, musical instruments, and fabrics were everyday necessities for self-reliant pioneers. Children played with toys such as dolls and gee-haw-whimmy-diddles. The rich frontier heritage continues today as many traditional arts and crafts have been handed down through the generations. Today, these art forms are also studied at various schools throughout the region.

**Complete these sentences.**

Without furniture, I couldn't

______________________________________________________________

______________________________________________________________

Without songwriters, I couldn't

______________________________________________________________

______________________________________________________________

Without clothing, I couldn't

______________________________________________________________

______________________________________________________________

Without electronic equipment, I couldn't

______________________________________________________________

______________________________________________________________

# Tennessee Word Wheel!

**Use the Word Wheel of Tennessee names to complete the sentences below.**

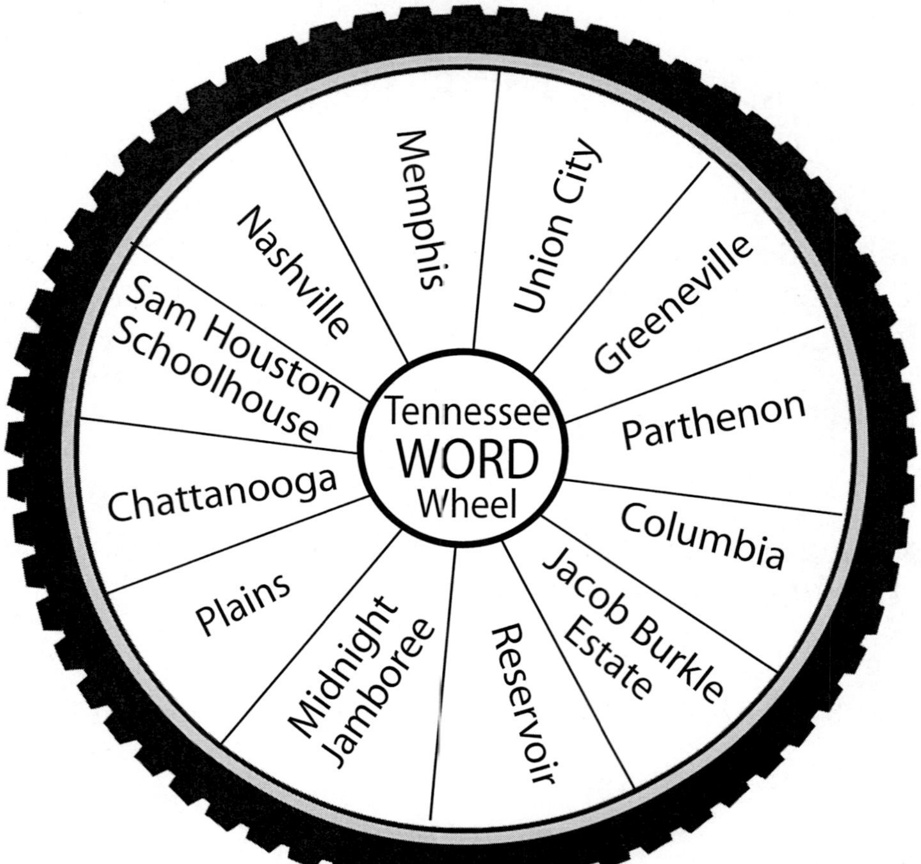


1. The _ _ _ _ _ _ _ _ _ is located in Nashville.
2. Graceland is the _ _ _ _ _ _ _ home of Elvis Presley. It's the second most visited house in the United States. (The White House is Number One!)
3. You can see a great show at the Ernest Tubb _ _ _ _ _ _ _ _ _ _ _ _ _ _ _ _ in Nashville.
4. The _ _ _ _ _ _ _ _ _ _ _ _ _ _ _ _ _ _ in Memphis was a "station" for slaves making their escape to freedom on the Underground Railroad!
5. James K. Polk Ancestral Home in _ _ _ _ _ _ _ _ was built in 1816. It's the home where James K. Polk began his legal and political career.
6. Tennessee's first public library opened its doors in 1813 in the city of _ _ _ _ _ _ _ _ _.
7. The National Medal of Honor Museum of Military History in _ _ _ _ _ _ _ _ _ _ _ is a very inspiring place to visit!
8. The first monument to honor an unknown soldier of the Confederacy is located in _ _ _ _ _ _ _ _ _.
9. The _ _ _ _ _ _ _ _ _ _ _ _ _ _ _ _ _ _ _ _ _ _ in Maryville is named for the great statesman and pioneer who taught there in 1812.
10. The only war monument in the United States that honors both the Confederate and Union armies is located in _ _ _ _ _ _ _ _ _ _ _.

**ANSWERS:** 1-Parthenon; 2-Memphis; 3-Midnight Jamboree; 4-Jacob Burkle Estate; 5-Columbia; 6-Nashville 7-Chattanooga; 8-Union City; 9-Sam Houston Schoolhouse; 10-Greeneville

# The Roads Well Traveled!

Tennessee has four major transportation hubs: Memphis, Nashville, Knoxville, and Chattanooga. More than 86,000 miles (138,400 kilometers) of highways wind their way through the state. Major interstate highways include: I-75, I-40, I-24, I-65, I-23, I-81, I-64, and I-51. I-40 is the main east to west route that links Tennessee's principal cities.

**Using the map below to help you, write down the direction you'd travel and the highway you'd take in order to get from:**

1. Memphis to Jackson = ______________________________
2. Knoxville to Nashville = ______________________________
3. Chattanooga to Nashville = ______________________________
4. Kingsport to Knoxville = ______________________________
5. Nashville to Cookeville = ______________________________

**ANSWERS:** 1-northeast on I-40; 2-west on I-40; 3-northwest on I-24; 4-southwest on I-81; 5-east on I-40

# Create Your Own Tennessee State Quarter!

Look at the change in your pocket. You might notice that one of the coins has changed. The United States is minting new quarters, one for each of the 50 states. Each quarter has a design on it that says something special about one particular state. The Tennessee quarter will be in cash registers and piggy banks everywhere after it's released in 2002.

**What if you had designed the Tennessee quarter? Draw a picture of how you would like the Tennessee quarter to look. Make sure you include things that are special about Tennessee.**

# Tennessee Law Comes In Many Flavors!

**For each of these people, write down the kind(s) of law used to decide whether their actions are legal or illegal.**

1. Bank robber ______________________
2. Business person ______________________
3. State park ranger ______________________
4. Tennesseans ______________________
5. Doctor ______________________
6. Real estate agent ______________________
7. Corporate president ______________________
8. Ship owner ______________________
9. Diplomat ______________________
10. Soldier ______________________

# Mixed-Up States!

**Color, cut out, and paste each of Tennessee's eight neighbors onto the map below.**

**Be sure and match the state shapes!**

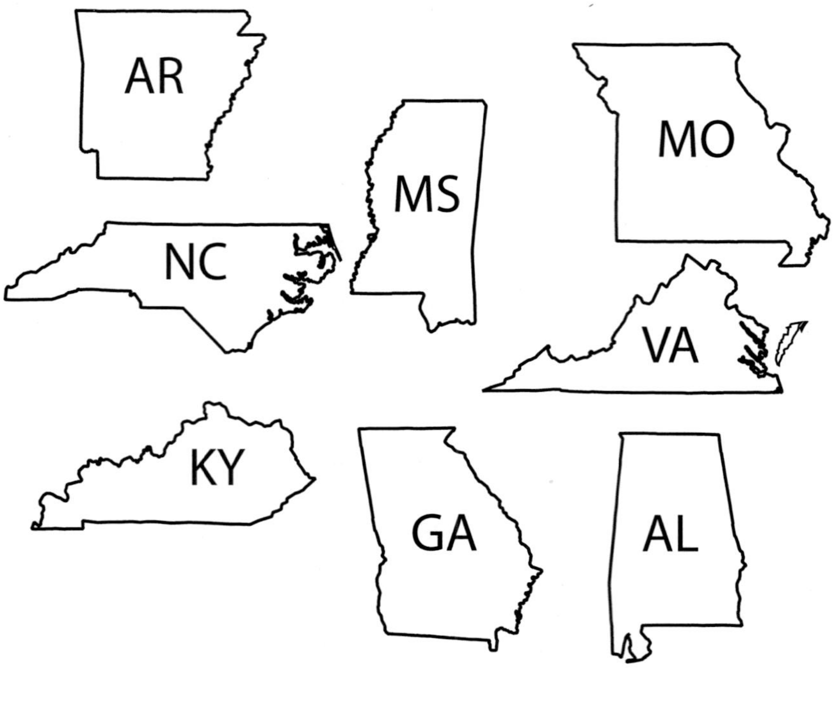

# Ahoy, Matey!

Memphis is Tennessee's main port, on the east bank of the Mississippi River. Memphis is one of the largest inland ports in the United States. Tennessee has 1,000 miles (1,609 kilometers) of navigable waterways including the Tennessee and the Cumberland rivers. The Tennessee-Tombigbee Waterway provides a direct route for ships sailing the Tennessee River all the way down to the Gulf of Mexico.

**When you're on board any kind of boat, you have to use special terms to talk about directions. Label the ship below with these terms:**

bow: front of the ship
stern: back of the ship
fore: towards the bow

aft: towards the stern
port: left as you face the bow
starboard: right as you face the bow

___ ___ ___ ___ ___ ___ ___ ___ ___

___ ___ ___ ___ ___

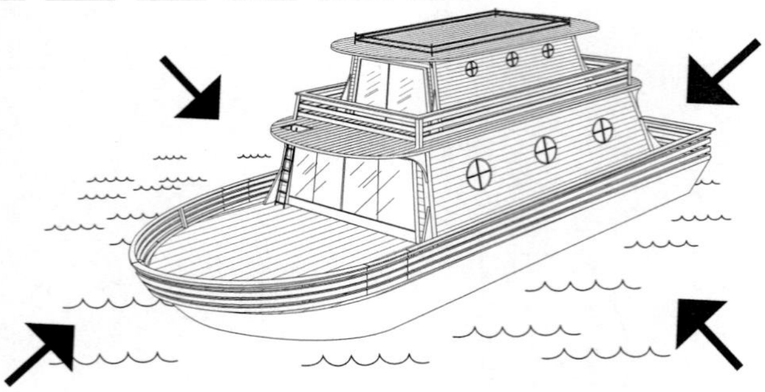

___ ___ ___

___ ___ ___ ___

This arrow is pointing ___ ___ ___ ___ .

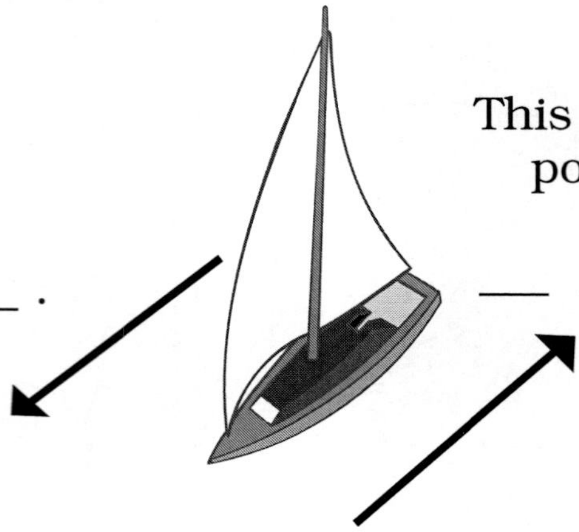

This arrow is pointing ___ ___ ___ .

# Tennessee Politics As Usual!

**On the lines provided, write down a question for each of the answers below. A hint follows each answer.**

Our elected government officials decide how much money is going to be spent on schools, roads, public parks, and libraries. Every election is important, and everyone who is eligible (able) to vote should do so!

Today, many elected government officials are women. However, before the 19th Amendment to the U.S. Constitution, women were unable to vote in national elections! In 1920, Tennessee was the 36th (and deciding) state to ratify the 19th Amendment, and it became the law of the land. Women gained total suffrage nationally and continue to be a major force in the election process today.

1. Question: ______________________________
   Answer: A draft of a law presented for review.
   (Short for William!)
2. Question: ______________________________
   Answer: The right to vote.
   (Don't make us suffer!)
3. Question: ______________________________
   Answer: The ability to forbid a bill or law from being passed.
   (Just say no!)
4. Question: ______________________________
   Answer: The fundamental law of the United States that was framed in 1787 and put into effect in 1789.
   (Tennessee has one too!)
5. Question: ______________________________
   Answer: An amendment.
   (It's not something subtracted from #4!)

**ANSWERS:** (may vary slightly) 1-What is a bill? 2-What is suffrage? 3-What is a veto? 4-What is the Constitution? 5-What is an addition to the Constitution called?

# What Shall I Be When I Grow Up?

Here are just a few of the jobs that kept early Tennesseans busy.

Longhunter
Lawyer
Tenant Farmer
Woodcarver
Judge
Housekeeper
Silversmith
Politician
Dairyman
Wheelwright
Teacher
Servant
Cabinetmaker
Mayor
Plantation Owner

Cooper (barrelmaker)
Carpenter
Weaver
Barber
Gardener
Mantuamaker (dressmaker)
Printer
Cook
Musician
Bookbinder
Laundress
Jeweler
Innkeeper
Stablehand
Tailor

Minister
Baker
Pharmacist
Gaoler (jailer)
Fisherman
Doctor
Governor
Milliner (hatmaker)
Soldier
Hunter
Blacksmith
Sailor
Beekeeper
Gunsmith
Prospector

**You are a young colonist trying to decide what you want to be when you grow up.**

**Choose a career and next to it write a description of what you think you would do each day as a:**

**Write your career choice here!** ______________________________

______________________ ______________________________

______________________________

**Write your career choice here!** ______________________________

______________________ ______________________________

______________________________

**Write your career choice here!** ______________________________

______________________ ______________________________

______________________________

**Write your career choice here!** ______________________________

______________________ ______________________________

______________________________

# Governor of Tennessee!

The governor is the leader of the state.

**You've been assigned to write a biography of the governor of Tennessee.**

**Before you can start your book, you need to jot down some notes in your trusty computer. Fill in the necessary information in the spaces provided on the screen!**

**GOVERNOR'S NAME:**

______________________________

______________________________

***Date of Birth:*** ______________________________

***Place of Birth:*** ______________________________

***Father:*** ______________________________

***Mother:*** ______________________________

***Siblings:*** ______________________________

______________________________

***Spouse:*** ______________________________

***Children:*** ______________________________

______________________________

***Pets:*** ______________________________

______________________________

***Schools Attended:*** ______________________________

______________________________

______________________________

***Previous Occupation(s):*** ______________________________

______________________________

______________________________

***Likes:*** ______________________________

______________________________

______________________________

***Dislikes:*** ______________________________

______________________________

______________________________

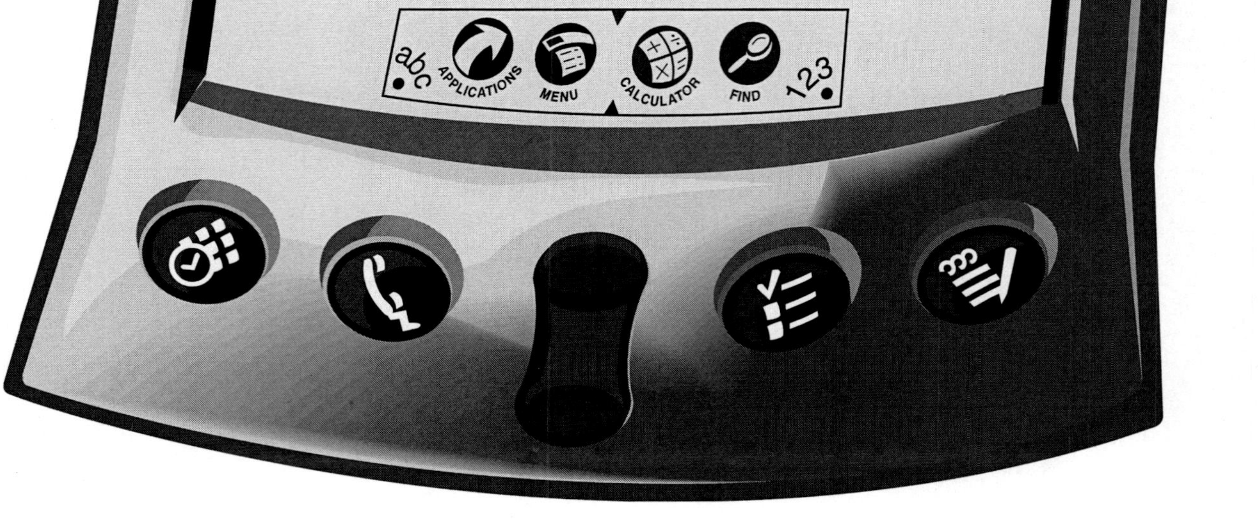

# The ORIGINAL Tennessee Natives!

Until recently, scientists believed that the first humans came to North America about 14,000 years ago. These people crossed over a land bridge between Siberia and Alaska, and then spread out across the North American continent. New evidence now suggests that people may have first arrived at the Americas 15,000, 20,000 or even 30,000 years ago! They were nomadic hunters who traveled in small bands and camped when seasons offered hunting, fishing, and fruit and nut gathering.

These prehistoric people were ancestors of the mound builders that lived in present-day Tennessee. Around AD 1000, farming began to replace hunting as the way of life for these early Tennesseans. The Mound Builders disappeared and were followed by tribes of Native Americans—Cherokee, Creek, Chickasaw, and Shawnee.

**What kinds of things did Native Americans use in their everyday life? For each of the things shown, circle YES if Native Americans did use it, or NO if they didn't.**

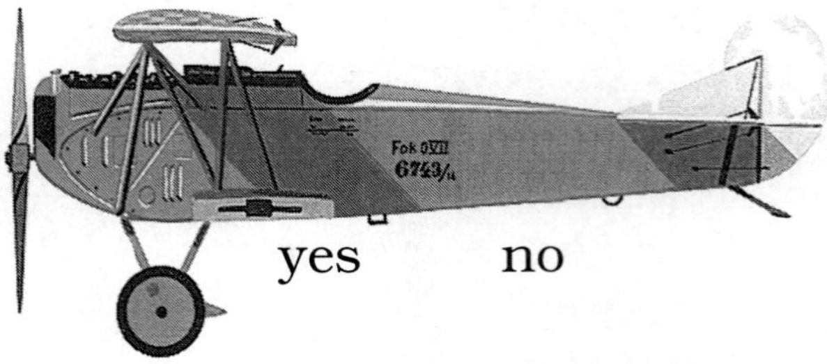


yes no

yes no

yes no

yes no

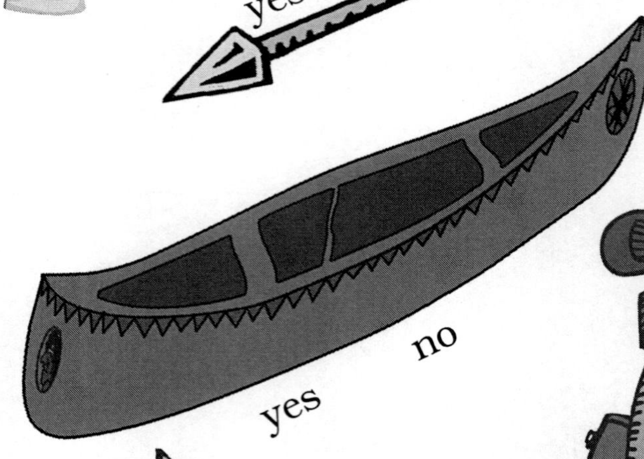

yes no

yes no

yes no

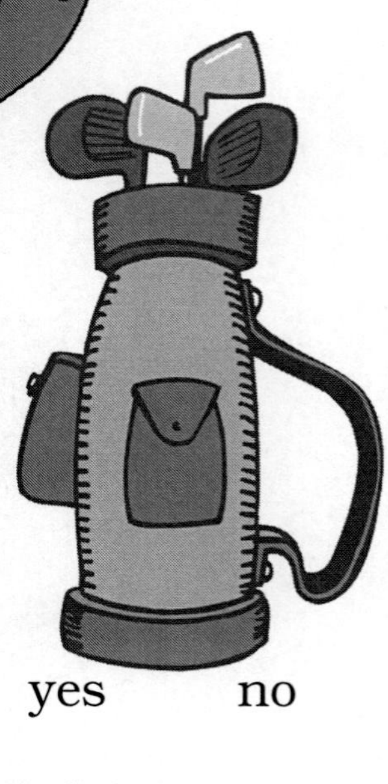

yes no

# States All Around Code-Buster!

**Decipher the code and write in the names of the states that border Tennessee.**

| A | B | C | D | E | F | G | H | I | J | K | L | M | N | O | P | Q | R |
|---|---|---|---|---|---|---|---|---|---|---|---|---|---|---|---|---|---|
| ✡ | ❀ | ✣ | ♣ | ✂ | ❤ | ✧ | ✎ | ☆ | ✆ | ☛ | ✹ | ✉ | ✪ | ➳ | ✦ | ✡ | ✲ |

| S | T | U | V | W | X | Y | Z |
|---|---|---|---|---|---|---|---|
| | | | | | | | |

1. ✧ ✂ ➳ ✲ ✧ ☆ ✡

2. ✶ ☆ ✲ ✧ ☆ ✪ ☆ ✡

3. ✡ ✹ ✡ ❀ ✡ ✉ ✡

4. ✉ ☆ ✳ ✳ ➳ ➳ ✲ ☆

5. ✡ ✲ ☛ ✡ ✪ ✳ ✡ ✳

6. ✉ ☆ ✳ ✳ ☆ ✳ ✳ ☆ ✦ ✦ ☆

7. ☛ ✂ ✪ ☎ ➳ ✣ ☛ ✠

8. ✪ ➳ ✲ ☎ ✎ ✣ ✡ ✲ ➳ ✹ ☆ ✪ ✡

**ANSWERS:** 1-Georgia; 2-Virginia; 3-Alabama; 4-Missouri; 5-Arkansas; 6-Mississippi; 7-Kentucky; 8-North Carolina

# Unique Tennessee Place Names!

**Can you figure out the compound words that make up the names of these Tennessee places?**

| | | |
|---|---|---|
| Bakewell | ________ | ________ |
| Beechgrove | ________ | ________ |
| Coldwater | ________ | ________ |
| Collegedale | ________ | ________ |
| Daylight | ________ | ________ |
| Ducktown | ________ | ________ |
| Eastland | ________ | ________ |
| Friendship | ________ | ________ |
| Goodspring | ________ | ________ |
| Greenback | ________ | ________ |
| Kingsport | ________ | ________ |
| Overall | ________ | ________ |
| Sweetwater | ________ | ________ |
| Turtletown | ________ | ________ |
| Whiteside | ________ | ________ |

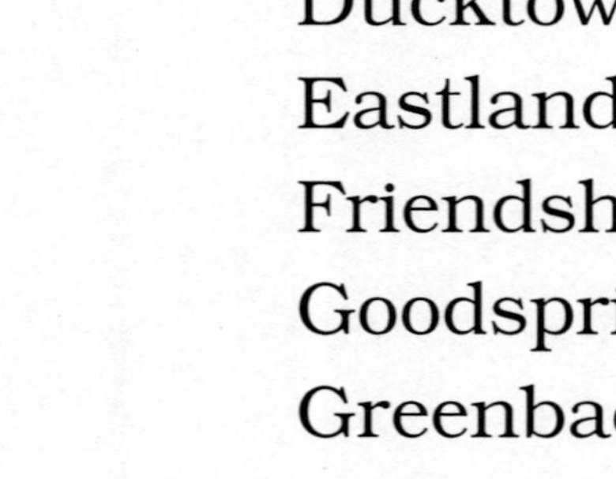

# Looking For a Home in Tennessee!

**Starting with the first, circle every other letter (or number) to check out the wildlife of Tennessee!**

1. More than _ _ _ species of birds and mammals live in the great state of Tennessee! (3 6 0 1 0)

2. The Great Smoky Mountains provide a home for many different types of animals including _ _ _ _ _ _ _ _, deer, black bears, and wild boars. (R O A F C E C S O M O A N P S)

3. Tennessee's rolling hills, fields, and forests are home to skunks, beavers, muskrats, rabbits, and _ _ _ _ _. (F I O W X T E F S)

4. Ducks, geese, quail, and _ _ _ _ _ _ _ _ _ _ _ _ are popular game birds. (W E I O L S D T O U W R C K P E X Y L S)

5. Bass, crappies, catfish, walleyes, bream, trout, and _ _ _ _ _ _ _ _ _ swim in Tennessee's rivers, lakes, and streams.
(B B L P U X E H G S I O L M L A S)

6. Songbirds heard throughout the state include robins, eastern bluebirds, cardinals, wood thrushes, and
_ _ _ _ _ _ _ _ _ _ _ _.
(M I O V C E K A I X N F G M B E I W R L D K S)

**ANSWERS:** 1-300; 2-raccoons; 3-foxes; 4-wild turkeys; 5-bluegills; 6-mockingbirds

# I Love Tennessee, Weather or Not!

Tennessee has hot muggy summers, mild winters, and plenty of rain. Snowfall is light in Middle and West Tennessee, but the mountains of East Tennessee may get heavy snows. Temperatures can drop to an average of 28°F (-2°C) in the winter and rise to an average of 92°F (33°C) in the summer.

The record high temperature of 113°F (45°C), blazed its way through Perryville, on August 9, 1930. Folks in Mountain City felt the frost bite as the temperature reached its lowest reading -32°F (-35°C), on December 30, 1917.

**Seek Shelter Immediately!**

In March 1952, 67 people die and 282 are injured as 10 tornadoes tear through Tennessee. Damages exceed $5.5 million!

**The Big Quake!**

During the winter of 1811-1812, violent earthquakes erupt and change the northwestern Tennessee landscape. A crack opens between the Mississippi River and Cypress Bottoms. For three days during the quakes, the Mississippi River flows backward and fills the bottoms, creating Reelfoot Lake.

**On the thermometer gauges below, color the mercury red (°F) to show the hottest temperature ever recorded in Tennessee. Color the mercury blue (°F) to show the coldest temperature ever recorded in Tennessee.**

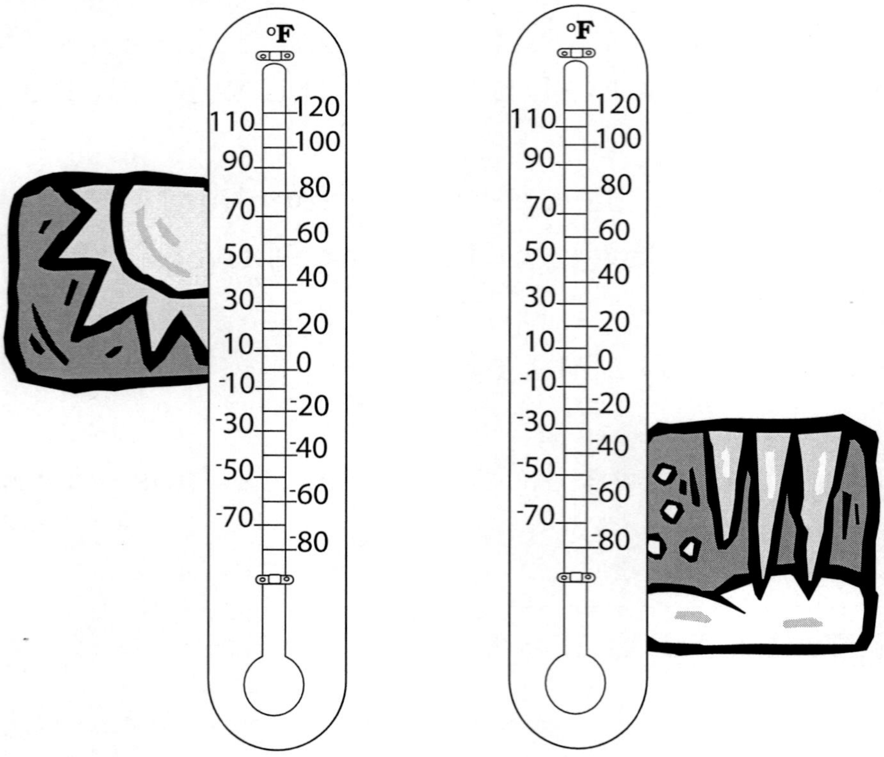

# The Scenic Route

Imagine that you've planned an exciting exploratory expedition around Tennessee for your classmates. You've chosen some cities and other places to take your friends.

**Circle these sites and cities on the map below, then number them in the order you would visit if you were traveling east to west through the state:**

__________ Natchez Trace State Park, Lexington
__________ Casey Jones Home and Railroad Museum, Jackson
__________ Center for Southern Folklore, Beale Street, Memphis
__________ Fort Nashborough, Nashville
__________ Blount Mansion, Knoxville
__________ Stones River National Battlefield, near Murfreesboro
__________ Great Smoky Mountains, East Tennessee
__________ Children's Museum of Oak Ridge

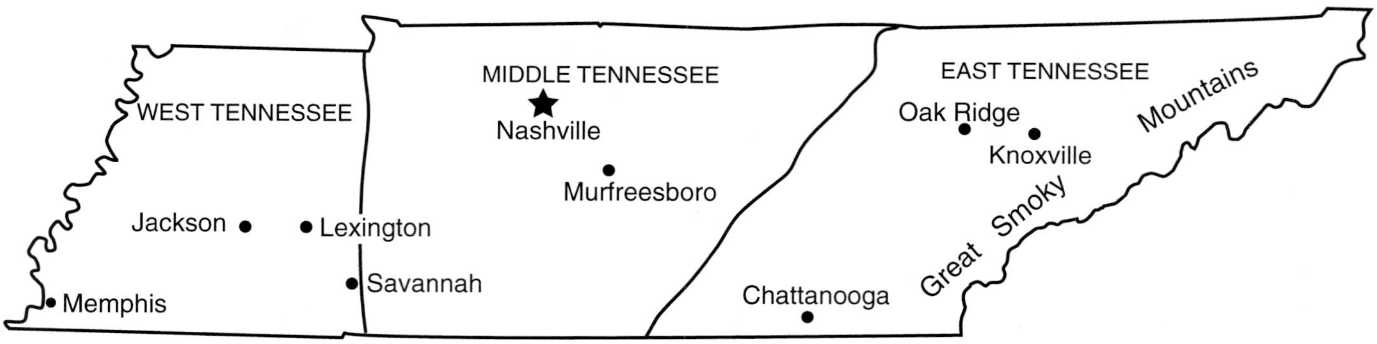

**ANSWERS** will appear in this order: 6; 7; 8; 5; 2; 4; 1; 3

# Key to a Map!

A map key, also called a map legend, shows symbols which represent different things on a map.

**Match each word with a symbol for things found in the state of Tennessee.**

airport (Memphis International Airport)

church (Saint Paul's Episcopal Church, Franklin)

mountains (Clingmans Dome)

river (Tennessee River)

riverboats (*Memphis Queen*)

road (I-40)

school (University of Tennessee)

state capital (Nashville)

battle site (Fort Donelson National Battlefield and Cemetery, Dover)

bird sanctuary (Hatchie National Wildlife Refuge)

# BROTHER, CAN YOU SPARE A DIME?

After the collapse of the stock market on Wall Street in 1929, the state of Tennessee, along with the rest of the nation, plunged headfirst into the Great Depression. It was the worst economic crisis America had ever known. Banks closed and businesses crashed...there was financial ruin everywhere.

In 1933, as part of the New Deal, the U.S. government created the Tennessee Valley Authority to help control floods, improve navigation, produce electricity, reforest lands, and encourage agricultural and industrial development. This federal act greatly improved the daily lives of Tennessee residents and created lots of jobs!

**Our President Helps**

While the nation was in the midst of the Depression, Franklin Delano Roosevelt became president. With America on the brink of economic devastation, the federal government stepped forward and hired unemployed people to build parks, bridges, and roads. With this help, and other government assistance, the country began to slowly, and painfully, pull out of the Great Depression. Within the first 100 days of his office, Roosevelt enacted a number of policies to help minimize the suffering of the nation's many unemployed workers. These programs were known as the NEW DEAL. The jobs helped families support themselves and improved the country's infrastructure.

**Put an X next to the jobs that were part of Roosevelt's New Deal.**

1. computer programmer ________
2. bridge builder ________
3. fashion model ________
4. park builder ________
5. interior designer ________
6. hospital builder ________
7. school builder ________
8. website designer ________

**ANSWERS:** 2;4;6;7

# Tennessee Newcomers!

People have come to Tennessee from other states and many other countries on almost every continent! As time goes by, Tennessee's population grows more diverse. This means that people of different races and from different cultures and ethnic backgrounds have moved to Tennessee. All Tennesseans benefit from this diverse culture!

In the past, many immigrants came to Tennessee from England, Scotland, Ireland, Germany, Wales, and Italy. More recently, Asians, Hispanics, and Pacific Islanders have migrated to Tennessee. The state is proud of its heritage, including Native Americans and African Americans.

Only a certain number of immigrants are allowed to move to America each year. Many of these immigrants eventually become U.S. citizens.

**Read the statement and decide if it's a fact or an opinion. Write your answer on the line.**

1. Many of Tennessee's early immigrants came from Europe.

   ______________________

2. Lots of immigrants speak a language other than English.

   ______________________

3. The clothing immigrants wear is very interesting.

   ______________________

4. Immigrants from England have a neat accent when they speak.

   ______________________

5. Many immigrants will become U.S. citizens.

   ______________________

6. People have immigrated to Tennessee from nearly every country in the world. ______________________

**ANSWERS:** 1-fact; 2-fact; 3-opinion; 4-opinion; 5-fact; 6-fact

# A Day In The Life Of A Settler

Pretend you are a settler in the days of early Tennessee. You keep a diary of what you do each day. **Write in the "diary" what you might have done on a long, hot summer day in July 1780.**

# This Old House!

Take yourself back 100 years. Can you imagine what life would be like in the Victorian Era? What did turn-of-the-century Tennesseans own? How did they live? See if you can pick out which of the following items people at the turn of the century had and which ones they did not.

**Circle the things you might find or use around your 1900 home.**

**ANSWERS:** 1, 2, 3, 4, 6, 7, 9, 10, 11, 13, 15, 16, 17, 18, 19, 20, 22

# Home, Sweet Home!

Tennessee has been the home of many different authors. Here are just a few. See if you can locate their hometowns on the map of Tennessee below! **Write the number of each author near the town where he or she lived. Some towns may be used twice.**

1. James Agee—author; won a Pulitzer Prize for his novel *A Death in the Family*; wrote screenplays including *The African Queen* (home—large city in East Tennessee on I-40 between Kingston and Morristown)

2. Mary Noailles Murfree—author; wrote under pen name of Charles E. Craddock; wrote *The Frontiersman*, *In the Tennessee Mountains*, and *In the Clouds* (home—southeast of Nashville, between Woodbury and Stones River National Battlefield)

3. Alex Haley—author; won Pulitzer Prize for *Roots*; collaborated on *The Autobiography of Malcolm X* (home—northeast of Memphis between Ripley and Covington)

4. Thomas Lanier Williams—famous playwright; chose pen name of Tennessee Williams for fond memories of childhood in Tennessee; wrote *A Streetcar Named Desire* (his childhood home sounds like a capital place to live)

5. Adolph S. Ochs—publisher; owner and publisher of *The Chattanooga Times* and *The New York Times*; coined the phrase, "All the news that's fit to print." (home—that same big city on I-40 where James Agee lived)

6. Ida B. Wells Barnett—African American educator, journalist, social reformer; fought for equal rights and to improve conditions for African Americans; editor of *The Free Speech* and *Headlight* (home—big city in the southwestern corner of the state on the Mississippi River, a blues kind of rockin' and rollin' city)

**ANSWERS:** 1-Knoxville; 2-Murfreesboro; 3-Henning; 4-Nashville; 5-Knoxville; 6-Memphis

# Tennessee Spelling Bee!

**Good spelling is a good habit. Study the words on the the page. Then fold the page in half and "take a spelling test" on the right side. Have a buddy read the words aloud to you. When finished, unfold the page and check your spelling. Keep your score. GOOD LUCK.**

- agriculture
- Appalachia
- Cherokee
- Chickasaw
- Choctaw
- Civil War
- Confederacy
- Creek
- East Tennessee
- firefly
- iris
- ladybug
- Middle Tennessee
- mountains
- music
- Nashville
- raccoon
- Shawnee
- Union
- West Tennessee

# Naturally Tennessee!

**Fill in the bubblegram with some Tennessee crops and natural resources. Use the letter clues to help you.**

**WORD BANK**
agate
barite
cement
coal
gravel
limestone
marble
petroleum
sandstone
zinc

Did you know water is a natural resource too? The Tennessee Valley Authority created most of Tennessee's lakes by building dams and locks on some of the state's rivers.

Forests cover about half the land area of Tennessee.

1. (C) ( ) __ __
2. __ __ ( ) C
3. __ __ __ D ( ) __ __ __ __
4. __ ( ) T ( ) __ __ __ __ __
5. __ __ __ (V) __ __
6. (A) __ __ __ E
7. __ __ M __ __ ( )
8. B __ __ ( ) __ __
9. L __ __ __ __ __ ( ) ( ) __
10. __ __ __ B __ __

**Now unscramble the "bubble" letters to find out the mystery word!**
**HINT: What is one way we can help to save our environment?**

__ __ __ __ __ __ __ __ __ __ __ __

**MYSTERY WORD:** conservation
**ANSWERS:** 1-coal; 2-zinc; 3-sandstone; 4-petroleum; 5-gravel; 6-agate; 7-cement; 8-barite; 9-limestone; 10-marble

# Gone Fishin'!

The Tennessee Valley Authority and the U.S. Army Corps of Engineers have created artificial lakes by building dams along the Cumberland and Tennessee rivers. These lakes have come to be known as the Great Lakes of the South!

**Put the names of some of Tennessee's great lakes in alphabetical order by numbering them 1 to 15.**

_______________ Reelfoot Lake

_______________ Barkley Reservoir

_______________ Cherokee Lake

_______________ Nickajack Lake

_______________ Chickamauga Lake

_______________ Dale Hollow Lake

_______________ Kentucky Lake

_______________ Norris Lake

_______________ Old Hickory Lake

_______________ Pickwick Lake

_______________ Lost Sea

_______________ Watts Bar Lake

_______________ Douglas Lake

_______________ Boone Lake

_______________ Fort Loudon Lake

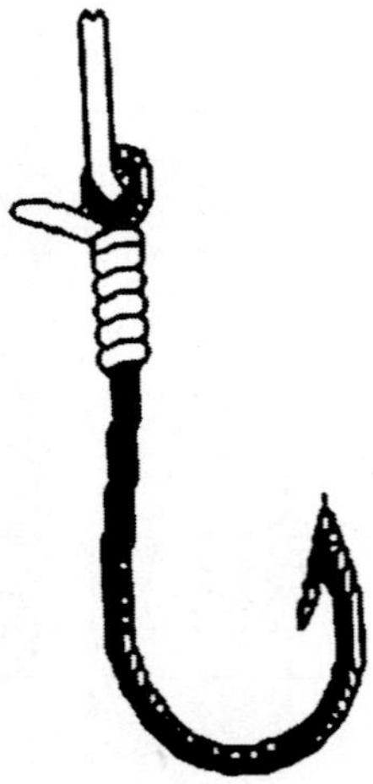

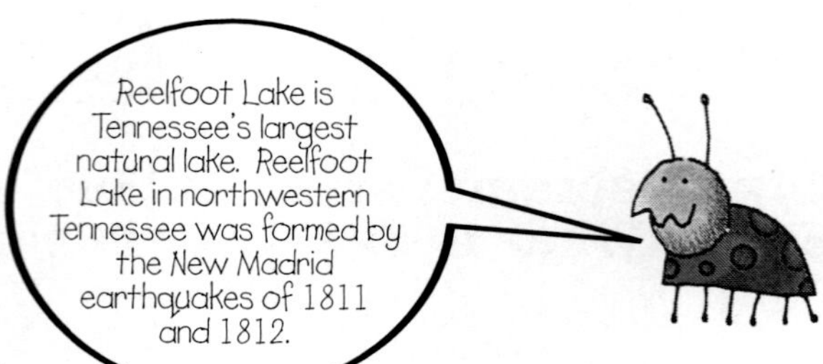

**ANSWERS** will appear in this order: 14; 1; 3; 10; 4; 5; 8; 11; 12; 13; 9; 15; 6; 2; 7

# What a Great Idea!

## WORD BANK

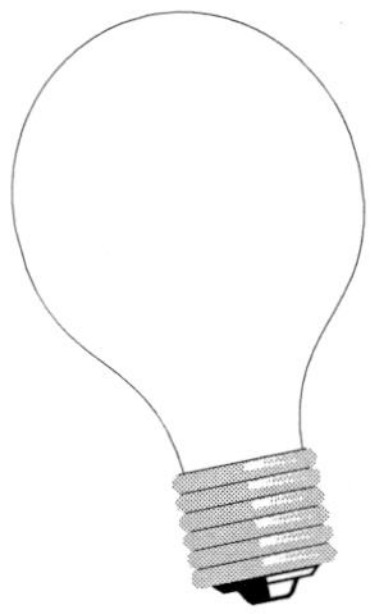

| | |
|---|---|
| Buddy | Piggly Wiggly |
| celestial | Seeing Eye |
| Cherokee | Sequoyah |
| Clarence Saunders | St. Jude Children's Hospital |
| Edward Barnard | written language |
| guide dogs | |
| Nashville | |

1. _ _ _ _ _ _ _ _ was a silversmith who created a _ _ _ _ _ _ _   _ _ _ _ _ _ _ _ for the _ _ _ _ _ _ _ _ Nation. He was the only man ever known to develop an alphabet on his own.

2. Astronomer _ _ _ _ _ _   _ _ _ _ _ _ _ discovered Jupiter's fifth moon and 16 comets. He was also a pioneer of _ _ _ _ _ _ _ _ _ photography.

3. Danny Thomas was an entertainer and humanitarian who founded _ _.   _ _ _ _   _ _ _ _ _ _ _ _'_   _ _ _ _ _ _ _ _ in Memphis.

4. The _ _ _ _ _ _   _ _ _ started in _ _ _ _ _ _ _ _ _ in 1928. It's the first U.S. organization to train _ _ _ _ _   _ _ _ _ for the blind. Morris Frank was the first American to have a Seeing Eye dog, and _ _ _ _ _, a German shepherd was that helpful dog!

5. _ _ _ _ _ _ _ _   _ _ _ _ _ _ _ _ of Memphis created the world's first supermarket and named it _ _ _ _ _ _   _ _ _ _ _ _!

**ANSWERS:** 1-Sequoyah, written language, Cherokee; 2-Edward Barnard, celestial; 3-St. Jude Children's Hospital; 4-Seeing Eye, Nashville, guide dogs, Buddy; 5-Clarence Saunders, Piggly Wiggly

# Famous Tennessee People

Here is a list of some of the famous people associated with our state. **Go on a scavenger hunt to see if you can "capture" a fact about each one. Use an encyclopedia, almanac, or other resource you might need. Happy hunting!**

William Bean ______________________________

Julian Bond ______________________________

Tracy Caulkins ______________________________

Charles Charleville ______________________________

David Crockett ______________________________

Timothy Demonbreun ______________________________

Julia Doak ______________________________

William Edmondson ______________________________

Elizabeth Gilmer ______________________________

Al Gore ______________________________

Tipper Gore ______________________________

Casey Jones ______________________________

Peyton Manning ______________________________

Robert Reese Neyland, Jr. ______________________________

Dolly Parton ______________________________

James Polk ______________________________

Wilma Rudolph ______________________________

John Sevier ______________________________

John Ward ______________________________

Ann Lee Worley ______________________________

# The Day It Rained SSSSSSnakes In Tennessee!

**Use the words from the Word Bank to fill in the blanks in this Tennessee legend. Some may be used more than once.**

**WORD BANK**
- frog-strangler
- ground
- Memphis
- rain
- sky
- slithering
- snakes
- *The New York Times*
- thousands
- weather

On January 15, 1877, the __________ in __________ took a strange, ______________ twist! Clouds rolled in and it began to _____. Not a gentle rain, but a torrential, ____-__________! Folks in the southern part of Memphis got more than rain—they got ______!

Over a few city blocks, snakes rained down. Not just a few and not just little ones! __________ of black snakes fell from the ___! Several days after the storm, there were still snakes slithering around on the ______.

The story got national attention, including a report in ___ ___ ____ _____. But so far, no one has come up with a really good explanation. What do you think caused this weird, wild weather phenomenon?

**ANSWERS:** weather; Memphis; slithering; rain; frog-strangler; snakes; thousands; sky; ground; *The New York Times*

# Map of North America

This is a map of North America. Tennessee is one of the 50 states.

**Color the state of Tennessee red.**

**Color the rest of the United States yellow. Alaska and Hawaii are part of the United States and should also be colored yellow.**

**Color Canada green. Color Mexico blue.**

Tennessee's magnificent scenery includes mighty mountains in the east that slope to lowlands along the Mississippi River in the west.

Welcome to the "Three States" of West, Middle, and East Tennessee!

Tennessee is one of the southern states.

LATITUDE: imaginary lines which run horizontally east and west around the globe
LONGITUDE: imaginary lines which run vertically north and south around the globe

# A State Bug Or Two, Or Three, Or Four!

Tennessee has two state insects, the firefly (*Photinus pyrallsis*) and ladybug (*Coccinella noemnotata*). Fireflies have a special light that shines white, yellow, orange, greenish blue, or red. In some types of fireflies, the females remain in the larvae stage and are called glowworms.

Ladybugs help Tennessee farmers by feeding on bugs that eat crops. In folk medicine, ladybugs were used as a cure for some types of diseases such as colic and measles.

Tennessee also has a state agricultural insect—the honeybee (*Apis mallifera*), and a state butterfly—the zebra swallowtail (*Eurytides marcellus*).

**Read each sentence, and decide if it is TRUE or FALSE. Write your answers on the lines provided.**

1. Tennessee has two state insects, a state agricultural insect, and a state butterfly! That's a total of four state bugs!

   ______________________________

2. Ladybugs have a special light that shines different colors.

   ______________________________

3. Glowworms are a type of firefly.

   ______________________________

4. Tennessee farmers don't like ladybugs because of the damage they do to crops.

   ______________________________

5. The state butterfly is used as a cure for some types of diseases.

   ______________________________

**ANSWERS:** 1-true; 2-false; 3-true; 4-false; 5-false

# Tennessee State Great!

**In the paragraph below about an important person from Tennessee, there are eight misspelled words. Circle the misspelled words, and then spell them correctly on the lines provided.**

*Nanye'hi* (Nancy Ward) was a Cherokee who foght bravely alongisde her husband at the Battle of Taliwa aganst the Creek. When her husband was killed, *Nanye'hi* rallyed the Cherokee warriors and lead them to victory! The Cherokee naimed her *Aqiqa-u-e*, or Beloved Woman, a title of honor given only too women of great influence. *Nanye'hi* served as a Cherokee leader for moor than 50 years.

______________________  ______________________

______________________  ______________________

______________________  ______________________

______________________  ______________________

**ANSWERS:** foght-fought; alongisde-alongside; aganst-against; rallyed-rallied; lead-led; naimed-named; too-to; moor-more

# Virtual Tennessee!

It's time to build your own website! We've given you pictures of things that have to do with Tennessee. Color and cut them out, and arrange them on a blank piece of paper to create a web page that will make people want to visit Tennessee!

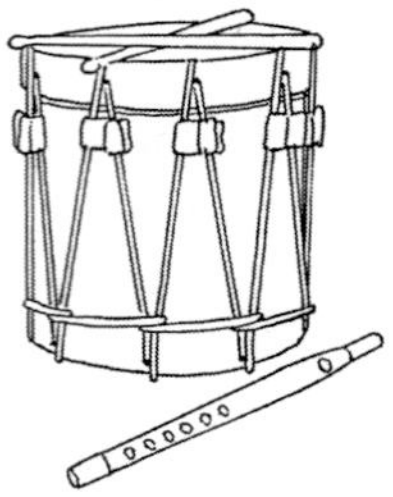

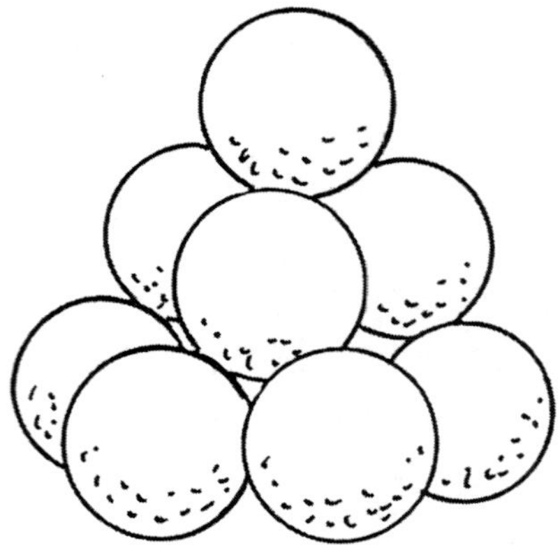

# A Lovely Lady Writes A Beloved Book!

Catherine Marshall was a woman of faith who was greatly influenced by a brave and loving mother. Her mother's life inspired Catherine Marshall to write a novel titled *Christy* about a sheltered city girl who left the security of her home to be a teacher in the Appalachian community of Cutter Gap.

Christy met the many challenges that awaited her with faith and courage. She came to know and love the proud people of Cutter Gap and their way of life in the Great Smoky Mountains.

Catherine Marshall's beloved novel *Christy* was made into a popular television series which was filmed in Townsend, Tennessee, in the Smokies.

**Read each sentence and decide if it is FACT or FICTION. Write your answers on the lines provided.**

1. Catherine Marshall was greatly influenced by her courageous mother. ________________________

2. Christy left her home in the city to be a teacher in the Appalachian community of Cutter Gap. ________________________

3. Christy was faced with many challenges in her new home. ________________________

4. Christy came to know and love the proud people of Cutter Gap. ________________________

5. The television series *Christy* was based on Catherine Marshall's beloved novel. ________________________

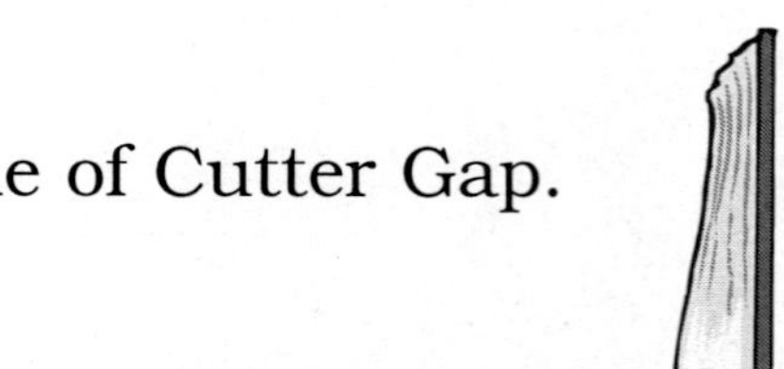

**ANSWERS:** 1-fact; 2-fiction; 3-fiction; 4-fiction; 5-fact

# A River Runs Through It!

The state of Tennessee is blessed with many rivers. See if you can wade right in and figure out these rivers' names! **Use the clues and the River Bank to navigate through the blanks.**

| RIVER BANK |
|---|
| French Broad |
| Little |
| Mississippi |
| Tennessee |
| Wolf |

1. _ _ _ _ _ _ _ _ _ _ _ River: The name of this river is spelled M-I-crooked letter-crooked letter-I-crooked letter-crooked letter-I-humpback-humpback-I.

2. This river could have appeared in "Little Red Riding Hood" or "The Three Little Pigs": _ _ _ _ River

3. _ _ _ _ _ _ _ _ _ _ River: This river shares the state name.

4. It's not the BIG river, it's the _ _ _ _ _ _ River.

5. This river sounds like a big, wide river in Europe: _ _ _ _ _ _ _ _ _ _ _ _ River

**ANSWERS:** 1-Mississippi; 2-Wolf; 3-Tennessee; 4-Little; 5-French Broad

# Tennessee Firsts!

**I'll trade you one Barbie for two Flintstones!**
The Box-A-Rama was held in Oak Ridge in 1990. It was the world's first lunch box collectors' convention.

**Yum!**
Little Debbie® Snack Cakes were first baked in 1960 by McKee Foods in Collegedale. Little Debbies were named after little Debbie, a granddaughter of the founder.

**Yum, too!**
Moon Pies® were first made in 1917 in Chattanooga. The Chattanooga Bakery Company bakes about 300,000 Moon Pies a day.

**Just gotta run in for a minute!**
In 1916, Clarence Saunders of Memphis created the world's first supermarket and named it Piggly Wiggly!

**Which "first" happened first?**

- Moon Pies® first made in Chattanooga
- Little Debbie® Snack Cakes first baked
- Piggly Wiggly's first store opening

The first "first" is: ____________________________________________

**ANSWER:** Piggly Wiggly's first store opening

# Tennessee Gazetteer

**A gazetteer is a list of places. For each of these famous Tennessee places, write down the town in which it's located, and one interesting fact about the place. You may have to use an encyclopedia, almanac, or other resource to find the information, so dig deep!**

1. Ryman Auditorium ____________________

   ________________________________

2. Tennessee Aquarium ____________________

   ________________________________

3. Bell Witch Cave ____________________

   ________________________________

4. Buford Pusser Home and Museum __________

   ________________________________

5. National Civil Rights Museum __________

   ________________________________

6. Pink Palace Museum and Sharpe Planetarium

   ________________________________

7. Fort Campbell ____________________

   ________________________________

8. Arrowmont School of Arts and Crafts ________

   ________________________________

**WORD BANK**

(cities may be used more than once)

| | |
|---|---|
| Adams | Gatlinburg |
| Adamsville | Memphis |
| Chattanooga | Nashville |
| Clarksville | |

**ANSWERS:** 1-Nashville; 2-Chattanooga; 3-Adams; 4-Adamsville; 5-Memphis; 6-Memphis; 7-Clarksville; 8-Gatlinburg

# Colonial Corn Husk Doll

You can make a corn husk doll similar to the dolls Tennessee settlers' children played with! Here's how:

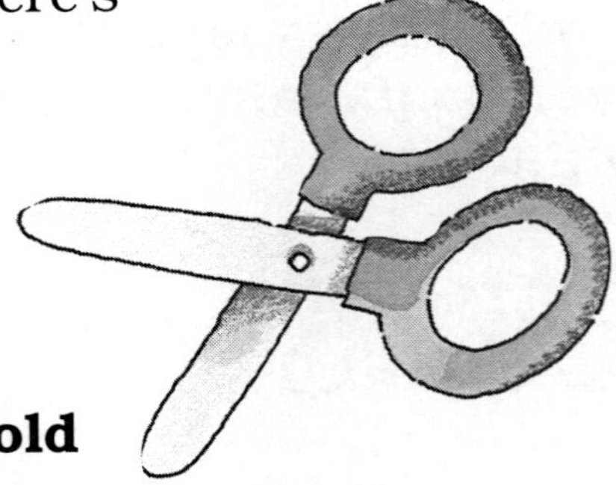

You will need:

- corn husks (or strips of cloth)
- string
- scissors

1. **Select a long piece of corn husk and fold it in half. Tie a string about one inch (2.54 centimeters) down from the fold to make the doll's head.**
2. **Roll a husk and put it between the layers of the tied husk, next to the string. Tie another string around the longer husk, just below the rolled husk. Now your doll has arms! Tie short pieces of string at the ends of the rolled husk to make the doll's hands.**
3. **Make your doll's waist by tying another string around the longer husk.**
4. **If you want your doll to have legs, cut the longer husk up the middle. Tie the two halves at the bottom to make feet.**
5. **Add eyes and a nose to your doll with a marker. You could use corn silk for the doll's hair.**

**Now you can make a whole family of dolls!**

# Tennessee Timeline!

A timeline is a list of important events and the year that they happened. You can use a timeline to understand more about history.

**Read the timeline about Tennessee history, then see if you can answer the questions at the bottom.**

|  |  |
|---|---|
| 1714 | French establish a trading post at French Lick. |
| 1763 | French and Indian Wars end. |
| 1769 | William Bean builds the first permanent European settlement on Boone's Creek. |
| 1775 | Richard Henderson forms the Transylvania Land Company and sends skilled woodsman and longhunter Daniel Boone to cut trails into the unexplored regions. |
| 1796 | Tennesseans adopt their first state constitution. |
| 1815 | Andrew Jackson and Tennessee volunteers defeat the British at the Battle of New Orleans. |
| 1818 | Jackson Purchase acquires Chickasaw lands. |
| 1838 | Cherokee are marched to Oklahoma on the Trail of Tears. |
| 1861 | Civil War begins; Tennessee secedes. |
| 1865 | Civil War ends. |
| 1866 | Tennessee is readmitted to Union. |
| 1925 | Scopes "Monkey" Trial takes place in Dayton; first Grand Ole Opry radio broadcast occurs. |
| 1968 | Martin Luther King, Jr. is assassinated in Memphis. |
| 2001 | Tennessee enters the 21st century! |

**Now put yourself back in the proper year if you were the following people.**

1. If you are listening to the very first broadcast of "Live from the Grand Ole Opry...," the year is ______________.
2. If you are a settler helping to build the first permanent European settlement on Boone's Creek, the year is ______________.
3. If you are a Tennessee volunteer fighting the British at the Battle of New Orleans, the year is ______________.
4. If you are a Cherokee being forced to leave your home and march to Indian territory in the West, the year is ______________.
5. If you are a reporter covering the famous Scopes "Monkey" Trial in Dayton, the year is ______________.

**ANSWERS:** 1-1925; 2-1769; 3-1815; 4-1838; 5-1925

# Tennessee State Economy!

Tennessee banks provide essential financial services. Some of the services that banks provide include:

- They lend money to consumers to purchase goods and services such as houses, cars, and education.
- They lend money to producers who start new businesses.
- They issue credit cards.
- They provide savings accounts and pay interest to savers.
- They provide checking accounts.

**Circle whether you would have more, less, or the same amount of money after each event.**

| | | | |
|---|---|---|---|
| 1. You deposit your paycheck into your checking account. | MORE | LESS | SAME |
| 2. You put $1,000 in your savings account. | MORE | LESS | SAME |
| 3. You use your credit card to buy new school clothes. | MORE | LESS | SAME |
| 4. You borrow money from the bank to open a toy store. | MORE | LESS | SAME |
| 5. You write a check at the grocery store. | MORE | LESS | SAME |
| 6. You transfer money from checking to savings. | MORE | LESS | SAME |

**ANSWERS:** 1-more; 2-more; 3-less; 4-more; 5-less; 6-same

# I Am A Famous Person From Tennessee

**From the Word Bank, find my name and fill in the blank.**

**WORD BANK**

Samuel Powhatan Carter
Cornelia Fort
Andrew Jackson
Andrew Johnson
John Ross
Sergeant Alvin York

1. I was the 17th U.S. president. I served Tennessee in offices at local, state, and federal levels. One of my last official acts was to pardon all Southerners who fought in the Civil War.
   **Who am I?** ______________________________

2. I am the only American to have been both an Admiral in the U.S. Navy and a General in the U.S. Army.
   **Who am I?** ______________________________

3. I was the hero of the Battle of New Orleans and the 7th U.S. president. I helped Tennessee become a state. My nickname was "Old Hickory."
   **Who am I?** ______________________________

4. I was chief of the United Cherokee Nation and president of the National Council of Cherokees. I resisted removal of my people from our homes in Tennessee by the U.S. government but finally led our nation to Oklahoma.
   **Who am I?** ______________________________

5. I was an aviator and the first woman pilot to die serving my country. I was killed in a mid-air collision during World War II.
   **Who am I?** ______________________________

6. I was a soldier and humanitarian. I was a World War I hero who used effective combat tactics. I received the Medal of Honor.
   **Who am I?** ______________________________

**ANSWERS:** 1-Andrew Johnson; 2-Samuel Powhatan Carter; 3-Andrew Jackson; 4-John Ross; 5-Cornelia Fort; 6-Sergeant Alvin York

# Mounds Abound In Tennessee!

Mound Builders lived along the rivers of Tennessee about one thousand years ago. They built their homes and temples on top of large earth mounds. They built smaller mounds to bury their dead. Presents were placed at the burial sites, probably as gifts to help the dead in the afterlife.

You are an archaeologist digging into the mound near Pinson in southwestern Tennessee. Below are pictures of some of the artifacts that you find. Now, you have to identify these strange objects and their uses.

**Write down what you think these things are for!**

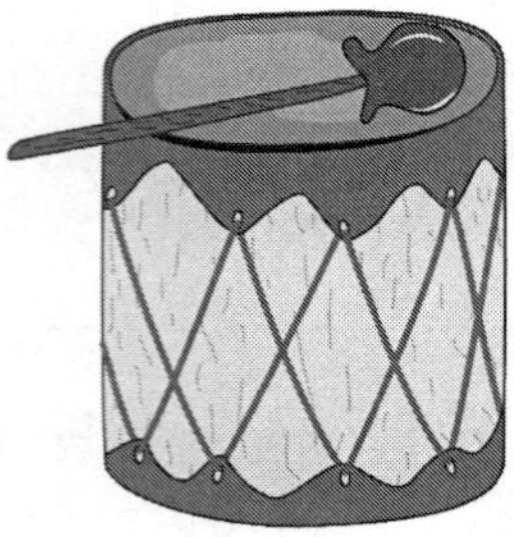

# Tennessee Native Americans!

When the settlers arrived in Tennessee, there were several Native American groups already living there—Cherokee, Creek, and Chickasaw.

The Cherokee lived in the northern part of East and Middle Tennessee. The Creek made their homes in southeastern Tennessee, and the Chickasaws lived in West Tennessee.

**Draw a line from each group to its location on the map.**

**Cherokee** **Creek** **Chickasaw**

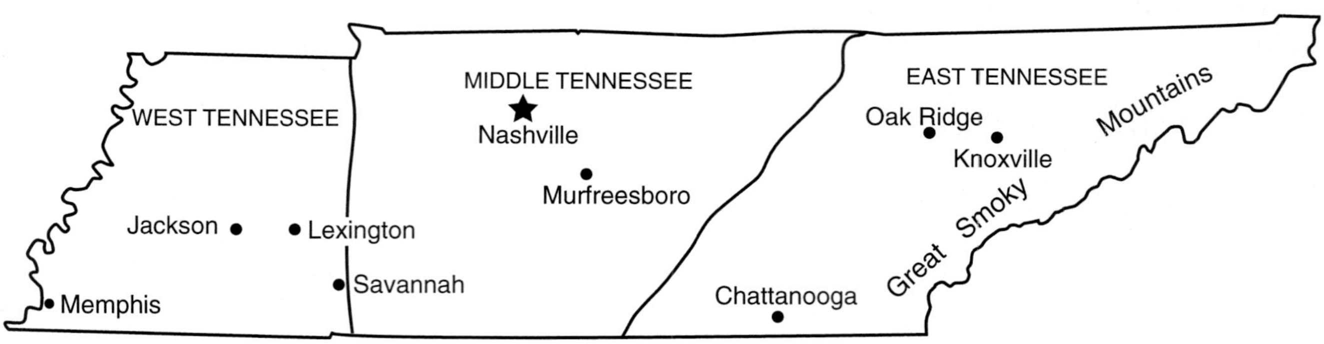

# IT'S MONEY IN THE BANK!!

You spent the summer working at Dollywood in Pigeon Forge, and you made a lot of money...$500 to be exact!

**Solve the math problems below.**

TOTAL EARNED: $500.00

I will pay back my Mom this much for money I borrowed when I first started working. Thanks, Mom! A. $20.00

subtract A from $500 B. ___________

I will give my little brother this much money for taking my phone messages while I was at work: C. $10.00

subtract C from B D. ___________

I will spend this much on a special treat or reward for myself: E. $25.00

subtract E from D F. ___________

I will save this much for college: G. $300.00

subtract G from F H. ___________

I will put this much in my new savings account so I can buy school clothes: I. $100.00

subtract I from H J. ___________

TOTAL STILL AVAILABLE (use answer J) ___________

TOTAL SPENT (add A, C, and E) ___________

**ANSWERS:** B.$480 D.$470 F.$445 H.$145 J.$45 total available: $45 total spent: $55

# Take A Tour Of These Terrific Tennessee Towns!

WORD BANK

Bristol
Chattanooga
Clarksville
Columbia
Gatlinburg
Goodlettsville
Greeneville
Jackson

Johnson City
Kingsport
Knoxville
Memphis
Murfreesboro
Nashville
Oak Ridge

E C J C E T D B U E I A J G O

S L F O S L R L G A G P A R B

T F L O H I L D W O T T C E O

R M V I S N I I O C L I K E R

O H E T V R S N V I Q L S N O

P E O M K S A O N X K Q O E B

S L K A P T T B N M O B N V S

G C O C T H U T O C V N H I E

N K E A O R I R E W I K K L E

I I H D G N P S M L Q T I L R

K C M C P S Q B T M D T Y E F

C L A R K S V I L L E O V L R

E L L I V H S A N O L H O Q U

K C O L U M B I A O A J U G M

I L F F G A O F J X U F K S T

# Numbering the Tennesseans!

STATE OF TENNESSEE

## CENSUS REPORT

Every ten years, it's time for Tennesseans to stand up and be counted. Since 1790, the United States has conducted a census, or count, of each of its citizens. **Practice filling out a pretend census form.**

Name ______________________________ Age [ ]

Place of Birth ____________________________________

Current Address ____________________________________

Does your family own or rent where you live? ________________

How long have you lived in Tennessee? ____________

How many people are in your family? ___________

How many females? [ ]   How many males? [ ]

What are their ages? ______________

How many rooms are in your house? [ ]

How is your home heated? ________________

How many cars does your family own? [ ]

How many telephones are in your home? [ ]

Is your home a farm? __________

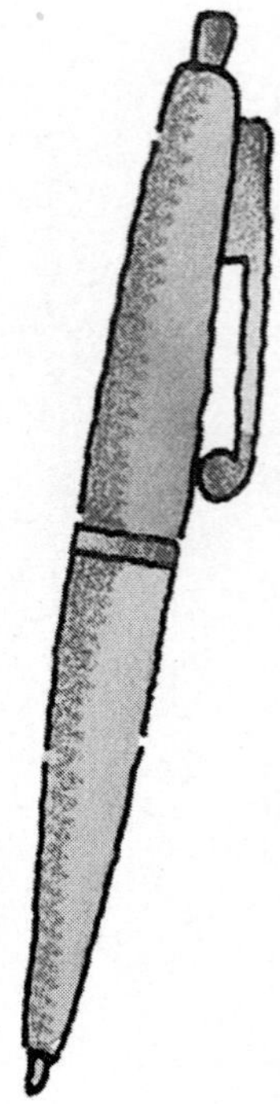

Sounds pretty nosy, doesn't it? But a census is very important. The information is used for all kinds of purposes, including setting budgets, zoning land, determining how many schools to build, and much more. The census helps Tennessee leaders plan for the future needs of its citizens. Hey, that's you!!

# Endangered and Threatened Tennessee

Each state has a list of the endangered species found within its borders. An animal is labeled endangered when it is at risk of becoming extinct, or dying out completely. Land development, changes in climate and weather, and changes in the number of predators are all factors that can cause an animal to become extinct. Today many states are passing laws to help save animals on the endangered species list.

**WORD BANK**

American peregrine falcon
Anthony's riversnail
Nashville crayfish
red wolf
red-cockaded woodpecker

**Can you help rescue these endangered and threatened animals by filling in their names below?**

1. N __ __ __ v __ __ __ __   c __ __ __ f __ __ __

2. r __ __-__ __ __ __ a __ __ __   w __ __ __ __ e __ __ __ r

3. __ e __   w __ __ __

4. __ __ e __ __ c __ __   p __ __ __ g __ __ __ __   __ a __ c __ __

5. A __ t __ __ __ __'s   __ __ v __ __ s __ __ __ __

**Circle the animal that is extinct (not here anymore).**

**ANSWERS:** 1-Nashville crayfish; 2-red-cockaded woodpecker; 3-red wolf; 4-American peregrine falcon; 5-Anthony's riversnail

# Sing A State Song!

Here's the first verse and chorus of one of Tennessee's many state songs. Read or sing it, then answer the questions about this great state song!

**"Rocky Top"**
by Boudleaux and Felice Bryant

Wish that I was on ol' Rocky Top,
down in the Tennessee hills;
Ain't so smoggy smoke on Rocky Top;
Ain't no telephone bills;
Once I had a girl on Rocky Top;
Half bear, other half cat;
Wild as a mink, but sweet as soda pop,
I still dream about that.

Rocky Top, you'll always be
home sweet home to me;
Good ol' Rocky Top;
Rocky Top, Tennessee;
Rocky Top, Tennessee.

**Answer the following questions:**

1. Where is Rocky Top?

_______________________________________________

2. What's one of the things that doesn't exist on Rocky Top?

_______________________________________________

3. What's one of the animals the singer's girl is like?

_______________________________________________

4. How does the singer think about his girl?

_______________________________________________

5. What will Rocky Top always be?

_______________________________________________

**ANSWERS:** (may vary slightly) 1-down in the Tennessee hills; 2-smoggy smoke or telephone bills; 3 bear, cat, or mink; 4-in his dreams; 5-home, sweet home

# Getting Ready To Vote In Tennessee!

When you turn 18, you will be eligible to vote. Your vote counts! Many elections have been won by just a few votes. **The following is a form for your personal voting information. You will need to do some research to get all the answers!**

I will be eligible to vote on this date ____________________

I live in this Congressional District ____________________

I live in this State Senate District ____________________

I live in this State Representative District ______________

I live in this Voting Precinct ____________________________

The first local election I can vote in will be ____________

The first state election I can vote in will be ____________

The first national election I can vote in will be _______

The governor of our state is _____________________________

One of my state senators is ______________________________________________

One of my state representatives is ________________________________________

The local public office I would like to run for is ____________________________

The state public office I would like to run for is ____________________________

The federal public office I would like to run for is __________________________

# The Tennessee State Seal

The state seal of Tennessee features the state motto and pictures of a plow, a boat, wheat, and cotton. The Roman numeral XVI stands for Tennessee being the 16th state, and 1796 is the date of the state constitution.

**Color the state seal.**

*MOTTO:* a sentence, phrase, or word expressing the spirit or purpose of an organization or group

Tennessee's state motto is "Agriculture and Commerce."

Tennessee has a state slogan, too! It's "Tennessee-America at its Best."

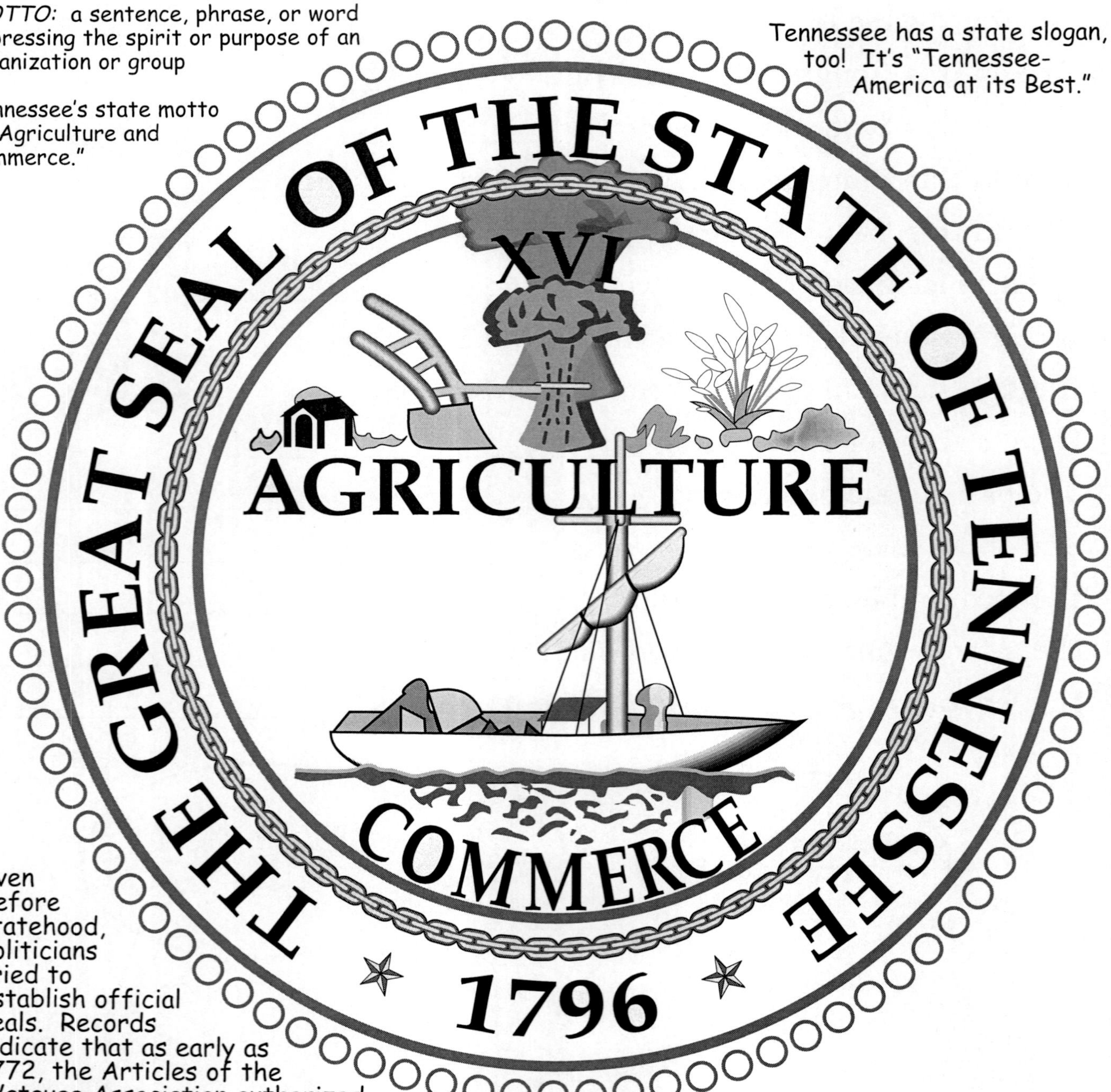


Even before statehood, politicians tried to establish official seals. Records indicate that as early as 1772, the Articles of the Watauga Association authorized the use of a seal.

# Tennessee State Symbol Scramble!

**Unscramble the names of these symbols for the state of Tennessee. Write the answers in the word wheel around the picture of each symbol.**

1. A R C C N O O
   HINT: furry mammals with bushy, ringed tails and black masks on their faces. They often live in dens in hollow trees.
2. G A L R E M T H O U  S S A B
   HINT: Tennessee's state sport fish lives in freshwater lakes, ponds, and streams throughout the state.
3. C N N A H E L  F C I A S T H
   HINT: Tennessee's state commercial fish. Sometimes known as the "spotted cat" or "fiddler," it's raised in farm ponds, and may be found in many lakes and streams.
4. K M O C I N G D I R B
   HINT: Tennessee's state bird lives in open country, farmlands, parks, and gardens. It can mimic other birds' calls. It can even make a sound like a dog's bark!
5. E T I H W B O B  L I A U Q
   HINT: The state game bird of Tennessee makes a sound that sounds like its name!

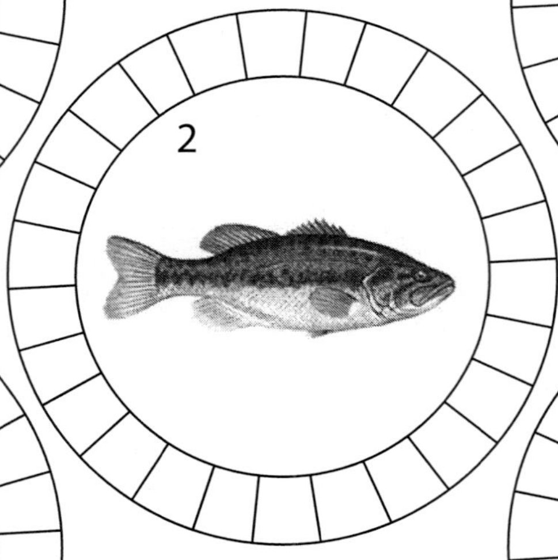

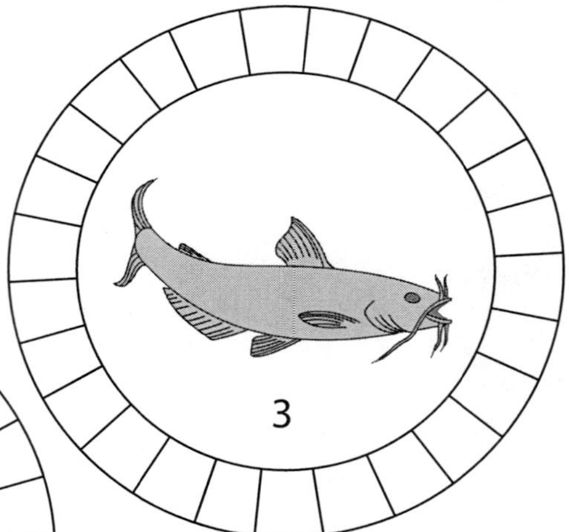

**ANSWERS:** 1-raccoon; 2-largemouth bass; 3-channel catfish; 4-mockingbird; 5-bobwhite quail

# A Quilt Of Many Counties

Tennessee is divided into 95 counties, most of which are governed by county courts (elected justices of the peace) and presided over by a county judge or chairman. Elected county commissions perform some counties' administrative functions.

- **Label your county. Color it red.**
- **Label the counties that touch your county. Color them blue.**
- **Now color the rest of the counties green.**

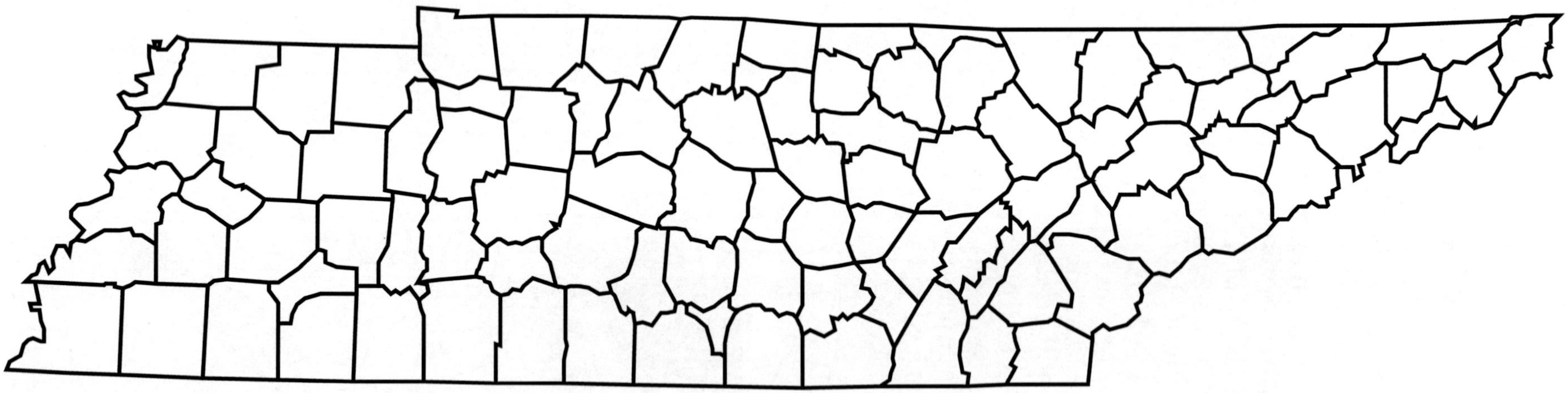

# Major Contributions!

W.C. Handy—blues musician and composer; known as the "Father of the Blues"; prestigious honor for blues artist, the W.C. Handy Award is named in his honor; best known song is "St. Louis Blues"; also wrote "Memphis Blues"; wrote blues songs on Beale Street in Memphis

Bessie Smith—powerful singer with a rich, deep voice known as "Empress of the Blues"; successfully blended African and Western music to create a distinctive "blues-jazz" sound

Nat Love—cowboy; most famous African American cowboy of the American West; earned nickname "Deadwood Dick" for shooting, roping, and riding skills

Dr. Martin Luther King, Jr.—civil rights leader, assassinated on April 4, 1968 in Memphis while in the city for a sanitation workers' strike to improve working conditions; National Civil Rights Museum located at the Lorraine Motel where Dr. King was killed

Sampson W. Keeble—first African American elected to General Assembly

Ted Rhodes—professional golfer; in 1961, broke through racial barriers prohibiting African Americans from playing in the Professional Golf Association

Wallace Saunders—an African American from Tennessee rode with Casey Jones and wrote "The Ballad of Casey Jones"—one of America's most popular folk ballads

**Read each statement about these important African Americans and decide whether the statements are FACT or an OPINION. Write your answer on the lines below.**

1. Dr. Martin Luther King, Jr. was an important civil rights leader.

   ______________________

2. Nat Love was the most rip-roaring cowboy ever!

   ______________________

3. Bessie Smith's powerful voice successfully blended African and Western music to create a distinctive "blues-jazz" sound.

   ______________________

4. If it had not been for the train wreck that killed Casey Jones, Wallace Saunders would never have written such a popular folk ballad.

   ______________________

**ANSWERS:** 1-fact; 2-opinion; 3-fact; 4-opinion

# Do You Believe In Ghosts?

One of Tennessee's most famous ghost stories is the tale (or tales) of the Bell Witch. "Kate" **tormented** the family of John and Lucy Bell, a **wealthy** couple who lived on a farm in Adams.

"Kate" slapped, pinched, and pulled the hair of family members, took covers off beds while people were sleeping, **recited** prayers, imitated the voices of local people, threw furniture, sang to visitors, and quoted scriptures from the Bible.

Andrew Jackson visited the Bell family to **confront** the famous ghost. "Kate" told the future president, "All right, General, I am on hand, ready for business!" And **apparently**, she was!

**See if you can figure out the meanings of these words from the story above.**

1. tormented: ______________________________

2. wealthy: ______________________________

3. recited: ______________________________

4. confront: ______________________________

5. apparently: ______________________________

HINT: You may need to look for the root word.

**Now check your answers in a dictionary. How close did you get to the real definitions?**

# Many Marvelous Musical Masters!

Tennessee is a land of music, music, music! East Tennessee has its Appalachian folk songs and bluegrass. Middle Tennessee is the home of country music, and West Tennessee created blues and rock 'n' roll.

Tennessee has many musical legends! The stars on this page are all "out of order." **Help them get back in line by putting them in alphabetical order!**

Amy Grant • Aretha Franklin • B.B. King • Bill and Gloria Gaither • Bill Monroe • Carl Perkins • Carter Family • Charlie Pride • Chet Atkins • Dolly Parton • Dottie West • Eddy Arnold • Elvis Presley • George Jones • Hank Williams (Sr. and Jr.) • Homer & Jethro • Howlin' Wolf • Jerry Lee Lewis • Johnny Cash • June Carter Cash • Kitty Wells • Loretta Lynn • Minnie Pearl • Muddy Waters • Patsy Cline • Porter Wagoner • Roy Acuff • Tammy Wynette • Tennessee Ernie Ford • Tina Turner

**ANSWERS:** Acuff; Arnold; Atkins; Carter Family; Johnny Cash; June Carter Cash; Cline; Ford; Franklin; Gaither; Grant; Homer & Jethro; Jones; King; Lewis; Lynn; Monroe; Parton; Pearl; Perkins; Presley; Pride; Turner; Wagoner; Waters; Wells; West; Williams; Wolf; Wynette

# It Could Happen— And It Did!

**These historical events from Tennessee's past are all out of order. Can you put them back together in the correct order? Number these events from 1 to 10, beginning with the earliest. (There's a great big hint at the end of each sentence.)**

_______ The first Nashville newspaper, *The Tennessee Gazette*, is published. (1787)

_______ The Indian Removal Act enables U.S. government to force Native Americans in the East to leave their homes and move west of the Mississippi River. (1830)

_______ The Watauga Association Constitution is written. (1772)

_______ The Civil War ends. (1865)

_______ *The Manumission Intelligencer*, the first antislavery paper in the United States, is published. (1819)

_______ The "Road Kill Bill" passes making it legal to keep and consume wild game, such as deer and bear, killed accidentally by vehicles. (1999)

_______ Tennessee creates a uniform system of public schools. (1837)

_______ Tennessee General Assembly passes a child labor law to protect kids who have to work outside of their homes! (1911)

_______ The U.S. Supreme Court rules that segregation is illegal in public schools. (1954)

_______ Tennessee becomes the 16th state. (1796)

**ANSWERS** will appear in this order: 2; 5; 1; 7; 4; 10; 6; 8; 9; 3

# Where's It Grown Or Raised?

Nearly one half of Tennessee is farmland. Soybeans and tobacco are the most important crops and grow in East and Middle Tennessee. Cotton grows in West Tennessee.

Livestock produces more than half of the state's income from agriculture. Cattle, hogs, and sheep are raised in Middle Tennessee where the grazing land is good for the livestock. The famous Tennessee Walking Horse is also raised in Middle Tennessee near Nashville.

**Label the crop or animal and draw a line to the spot in Tennessee where it's grown or raised.**

 ____________  ____________  ____________  ____________

 ____________  ____________  ____________

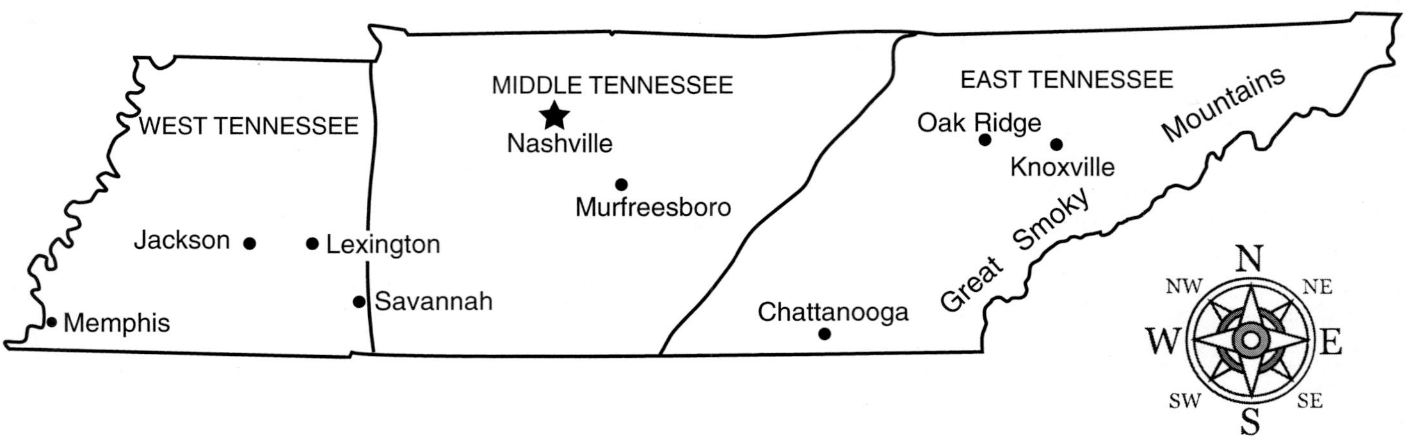

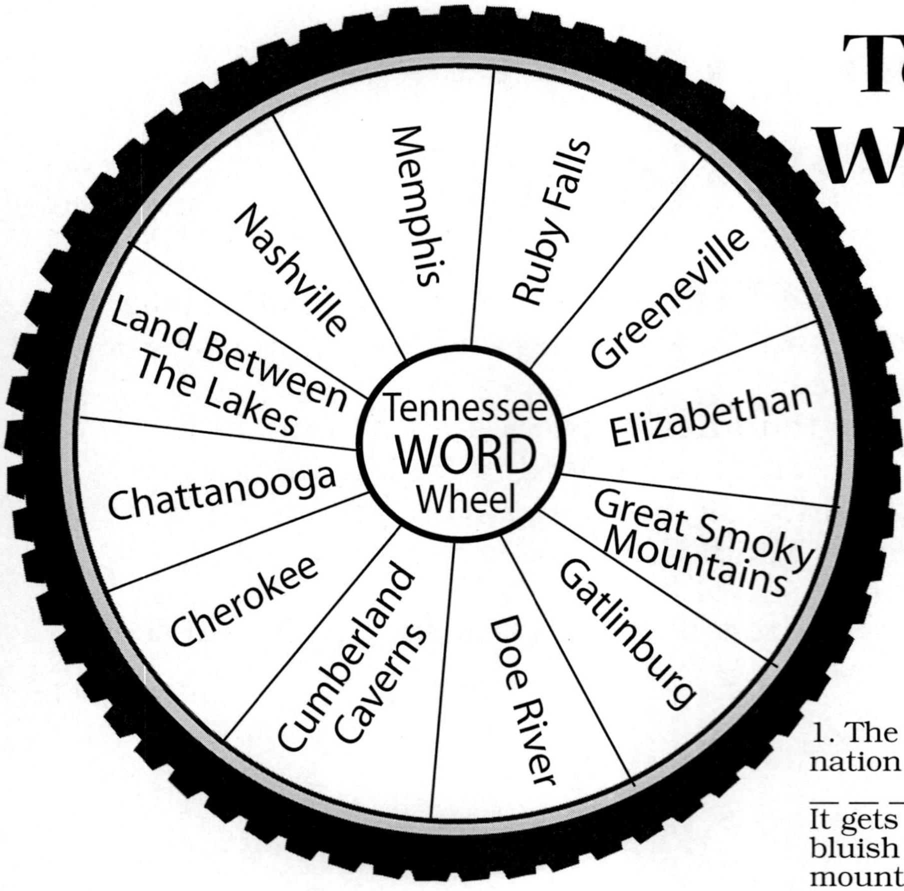


# Tennessee Word Wheel

## Give It Another Spin!

**Using the Word Wheel of Tennessee names, complete the sentences below.**

1. The most visited national park in the nation is the _ _ _ _ _ _ _ _ _ _ _ _ _ _ _ _ _ _ _ _ _. It gets its name from the smoke-like bluish haze that usually covers the mountains.

2. _ _ _ _ _ _ _ _ _ _ _ _ _ _ _ _ _ _ _ _ _ _ National Recreation Area near Dover has a living history farm, nature center, planetarium, trails, and lots more to enjoy!

3. The Carter Mansion in _ _ _ _ _ _ _ _ _ _ _ _ _ _ _, the home of John and Landon Carter, is one of oldest and most distinctive houses in Tennessee.

4. The State Library in _ _ _ _ _ _ _ _ _ _ _ has quite a connection to Andrew Johnson. When he was governor of Tennessee, he asked the legislature for money to start a new library. Today, the library has more than 250,000 volumes—many historical records that can't be found anywhere else!

5. _ _ _ _ _ _ _ _ _ _ in Chattanooga is a spectacular site below Lookout Mountain. And they're all natural! Don't forget to See Rock City!

6. The largest group of independent artists and craftsmen in the United States is the Great Smoky Arts and Crafts Community near _ _ _ _ _ _ _ _ _ _ _ _ _.

7. _ _ _ _ _ _ _ _ _ Covered Bridge in Elizabethton is thought to be oldest covered bridge in Tennessee still in use.

8. The Tennessee Aquarium in _ _ _ _ _ _ _ _ _ _ _ _ _ _ _ is the world's largest freshwater aquarium. There are 7,000 fish, birds, reptiles, amphibians, and mammals.

9. _ _ _ _ _ _ _ _ _ _ _ _ _ _ _ _ _ _ _ _ _ _ in McMinnville has the largest cave room in eastern America and a 3/4-ton (680-kilogram) crystal chandelier in the Volcano Room.

10. The Ocoee Whitewater Center in _ _ _ _ _ _ _ _ _ _ National Forest. The Ocoee River is rated one of the top white water recreational rivers in the United States. The Ocoee was the site of the 1996 Olympic white water canoe and kayak competition.

**ANSWERS:** 1-Great Smoky Mountains; 2-Land Between the Lakes; 3-Elizabethton; 4-Nashville; 5-Ruby Falls; 6-Gatlinburg; 7-Doe River; 8-Chattanooga; 9-Cumberland Caverns; 10-Cherokee

# Tennessee Pop Quiz!

**Pop quiz! It's time to test your knowledge of the great state of Tennessee! Try to answer all of the questions before you look at the answers.**

1. Tennessee became the ____th state in 1796.
   a. 16th
   b. 50th
   c. 14th

2. Which is NOT a nickname for the great state of Tennessee?
   a. The Volunteer State
   b. Big Bend State
   c. The Mother of Presidents

3. The stars on Tennessee's state flag represent three distinctly different regions. The Grand Divisions of the state are:
   a. North, South, and East Tennessee
   b. East, Middle, and West Tennessee
   c. Upper, Middle, and Lower Tennessee

4. Tennessee's state motto is:
   a. "Agriculture and Commerce"
   b. "Tennessee—America at its Best"
   c. "Tennessee—a Great Place to Visit"

5. Which Tennessee city is known as the "Country Music Capital of the World"?
   a. Memphis
   b. Nashville
   c. Knoxville

6. Tennessee's state tree is the:
   a. tulip poplar
   b. dogwood
   c. gum maple

7. The iris was chosen by the state legislature in 1933 to be Tennessee's cultivated flower. What is Tennessee's state wildflower?
   a. rhododendron
   b. mountain laurel
   c. passion flower

8. ____________ is a metamorphic (transformed) version of limestone and is used throughout the country to make monuments and buildings.
   a. old limestone
   b. quartz
   c. marble

9. Which mighty river forms the border between Tennessee and its two western neighbors—Missouri and Arkansas?
   a. Tennessee
   b. Mississippi
   c. Cumberland

10. Tennessee's Nashville Basin is similar to the Blue Grass Basin of Kentucky. Both regions are famous for raising:
    a. great-tasting crops
    b. fine horses
    c. taxes

**ANSWERS:** 1-a; 2-c; 3-b; 4-a; 5-b; 6-a; 7-c; 8-c; 9-b; 10-b

# Up In Arms!

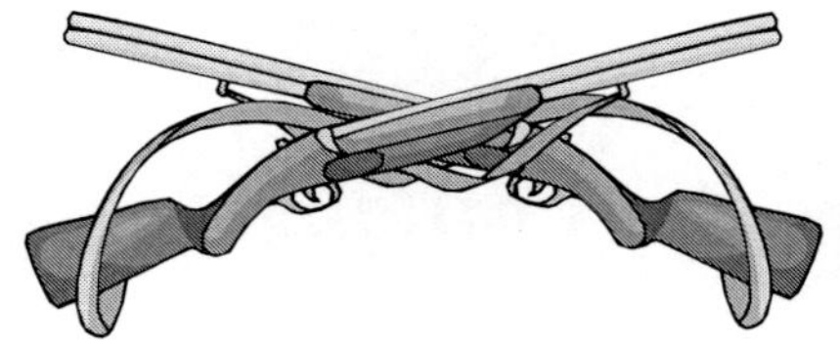

Some settlers in the New World felt that England ignored their ideas and concerns. In 1775, the colonies went to war with England. On July 4, 1776, the Declaration of Independence was signed.

Tennesseans fought bravely in the Revolutionary War against British and Loyalist troops and their Native American allies. In 1780, Tennessee riflemen fought and defeated British forces at the Battle of Kings Mountain in South Carolina, a major battle and turning point of the war in the South.

Following the Revolutionary War, North Carolina gave up its claim to Tennessee. Tennesseans made plans to form a new state called Franklin. But the new state of Franklin was short-lived as North Carolina reclaimed the Tennessee region.

**In each pair of sentences below, one of the statements is false. Read them carefully and choose the sentence that is not true. Cross out the false sentence, and circle the true sentence.**

1. Some settlers in the New World felt that England ignored their ideas and concerns. They wanted to sit down at the bargaining table and talk through the issues.

2. In 1775, the colonies went to war among themselves. On July 4, 1776, the Declaration of Independence was signed.

3. Tennesseans fought bravely in the Revolutionary War. They battled German troops and their Native American allies.

4. In 1780, Tennessee riflemen fought and defeated British forces at the Battle of Kings Mountain in South Carolina. It was a major battle of the war in the South that dragged on for many more years.

5. Following the Civil War, North Carolina gave up its claim to Tennessee. Tennesseans formed a new state called Franklin, but the new state of Franklin was short-lived.

**ANSWERS:** 1-second is false; 2-first is false; 3-second is false; 4-second is false; 5-first is false

# Massive Mounds Of Mighty Mountains!

There are more than 16 peaks in the Smoky Mountains that are taller than 6,000 feet (1,829 meters). Tennessee's tallest peak, Clingmans Dome, is the highest point along the Appalachian Trail that winds through the eastern United States from Maine to Georgia.

Tennessee's majestic Great Smoky and Unakas mountains include:

| | | |
|---|---|---|
| Clingmans Dome | 6,643 feet | (2,025 meters) |
| Roan Mountain | 6,285 feet | (1,916 meters) |
| Unaka Mountain | 4,840 feet | (1,475 meters) |
| Sampson Mountain | 4,060 feet | (1,237 meters) |
| Bald Mountain | 3,000 feet | ( 914 meters) |
| Mount Guyot | 6,621 feet | (2,018 meters) |
| Mount LeConte | 6,593 feet | (2,010 meters) |
| Cliff Top | 6,555 feet | (1,998 meters) |
| Mount Buckley | 6,500 feet | (1,981 meters) |
| Mount Love | 6,446 feet | (1,965 meters) |

**Using the information above, graph the elevations (heights) of these mighty mountains The first one has been done for you.**

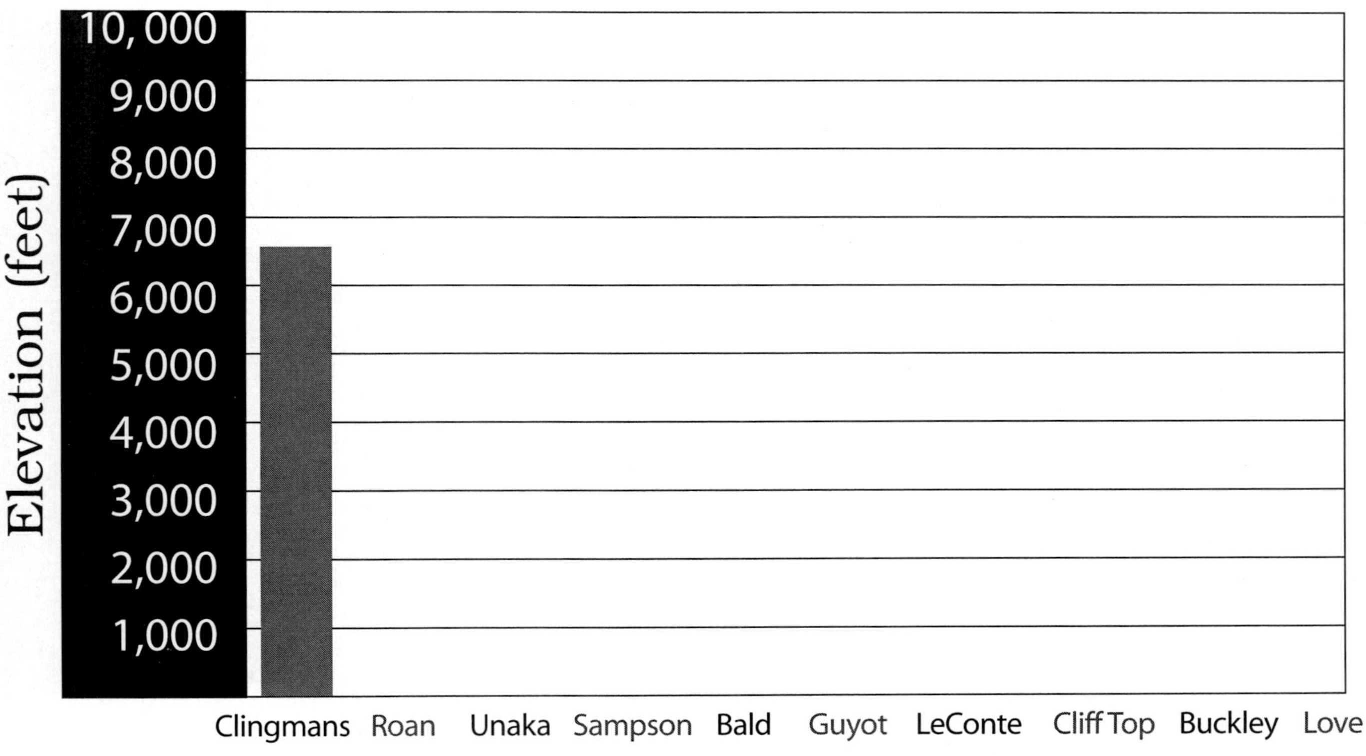

# What's In A Name? What's In A Haiku?

Tennessee got its name from a Native American word from the Yuchi language, *Tana-see* which means "The Meeting Place." Travelers in the 1700s associated the name with a Cherokee village and a river in Cherokee territory.

A haiku is a three-line poem with a certain number of syllables in each line. Look at the example below:

The first line has 5 syllables.
*Land/of/Vol/un/teers.*

The second line has 7 syllables.
*Lots/of/love/ly/sights/are/here!*

The third line has 5 syllables.
*Folks/come/to/be/near!*

**Now write your own haiku about the amazing state of Tennessee!**

________________________________________

________________________________________

________________________________________

# Time For A Hike!

The state of Tennessee is blessed with roaring rivers, lovely lakes, majestic mountains, wonderful waterfalls, and terrific trails. Everything a nature lover loves! In the Smokies alone there are more than 150 hiking trails, some dating back to long before the settlers came.

The Tennessee section of the Appalachian Trail extends for 72 miles (116 kilometers) across the crest of the magnificent Appalachian Mountains. More than 3 million hikers hike all or parts of the Appalachian Trail each year!

Throughout the great state of Tennessee hikers will find hundreds of trails to explore. Some are long. Some are short. Some are easy to climb. Some are hard. The "degree of difficulty" shows if the trail is easy or strenuous (really tough) to hike!

| Trail Name | Trail Distance | Degree of Difficulty |
|---|---|---|
| Hidden Passage Trail | 10 miles (16 km) | Moderate |
| North Ridge Trail | 7.5 miles (12 km) | Moderate |
| Honey Creek Loop | 5.5 miles (8.9 km) | Strenuous |
| Trail Angel Falls Trail | 2 miles (3.2 km) | Easy |
| Twin Arches Loop Trail | 5.9 miles (9.5 km) | Strenuous |
| The Paw Paw Trail | 5 miles (8 km) | Moderate |
| Rock Creek Trail | 5.5 mile (1.6 km) | Moderate |
| Fiery Gizzard Trail | 12.5 miles (20 km) | Strenuous |
| Pond Mountain Trail | 4.5 miles (7.2 km) | Strenuous |
| Sugarlands Trail | 1 mile (1.6 km) | Easy |

**Check out the chart showing a few of Tennessee's trails to find the answers to these questions.**

1. The longest trail on the chart is the _ _ _ _ _
   _ _ _ _ _ _ _ Trail.

2. Which trail is an easy 1-mile hike? _ _ _ _ _ _ _ _ _ _
   _ _ _ _ _

3. Which trail is closest to 6 miles? _ _ _ _   _ _ _ _ _ _
   _ _ _ _   _ _ _ _ _

4. Which trail is a strenuous 5.5 mile hike? _ _ _ _ _
   _ _ _ _ _   _ _ _ _   _ _ _ _ _

**ANSWERS:** 1-Fiery Gizzard; 2-Sugarlands Trail; 3-Twin Arches Loop Trail; 4-Honey Creek Loop Trail

# How Big is Tennessee?

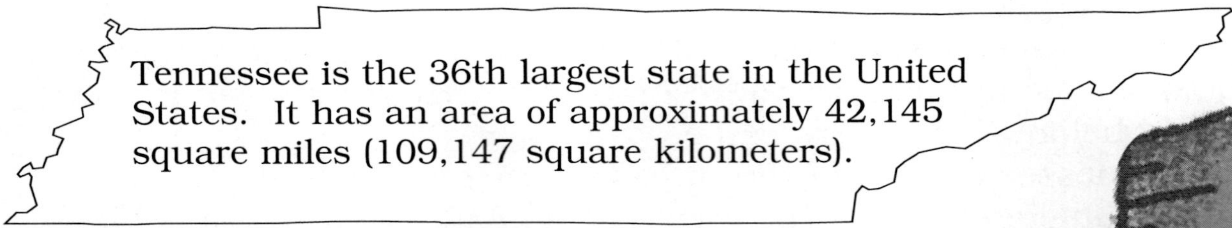

Tennessee is the 36th largest state in the United States. It has an area of approximately 42,145 square miles (109,147 square kilometers).

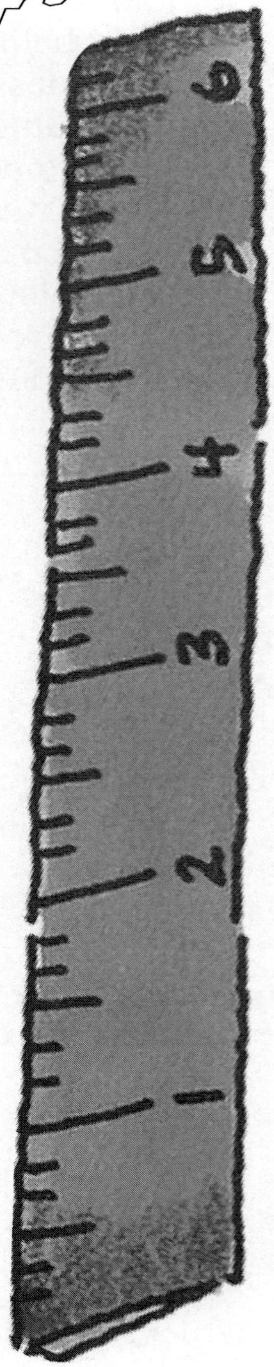

**Can you answer the following questions?**

1. How many states are there in the United States?

   ___________

2. How many states are smaller than our state?

   ___________

3. How many states are larger than our state?

   ___________

4. One mile = 5,280 _____ _____ _____ _____

   HINT: 

5. Draw a square foot.

6. Classroom Challenge: After you have drawn a square foot, measure the number of square feet in your classroom. Most floor tiles are square feet (12 inches by 12 inches). How many square feet are in your classroom? _____________

   **Bonus:** Try to calculate how many classrooms would fit in the total area of your state. _______
   Hint: About 46,464 average classrooms would fit in just one square mile!

**ANSWERS:** 1-50; 2-14; 3-35; 4-feet; 5-answer will vary; 6-answer will vary
**Bonus:** 1,958,225,280 classrooms!

# It's Time To Celebrate!

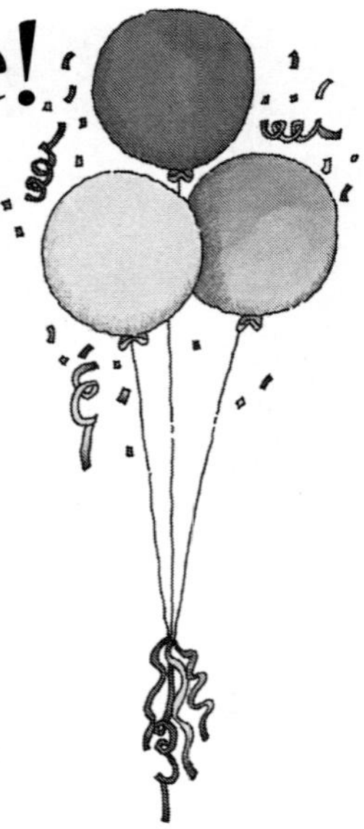

**Check out these great Tennessee fairs and festivals and answer the questions below!**

- Standing Stone Native American Celebration, Monterey
- Reelfoot Eagle Watch Tours, Tiptonville
- Great River Carnival, Memphis
- International Country Music Fan Fair, Nashville
- National Storytelling Festival, Jonesborough
- Mule Day, Columbia
- Old Time Bluegrass and Fiddler's Championship, Holla
- Dumas Walker (King of Marbles) Rolley Hole World Championship, Celina
- Dulcimer and Harp Festival, Crosby
- Tennessee State Fair, Nashville
- Upper Cumberland Quilt Festival, Algood
- Brownsville Blues Festival
- Smoky Mountains Winterfest, Gatlinburg, Pigeon Forge, and Sevierville
- Old-Time Fiddlers' Jamboree and Crafts Festival, Smithville
- Tennessee River Folklife and Music Festival, Eva
- Chester County Annual Barbecue Festival, Henderson

1. You have the "gift of gab" (that means you're a great storyteller), which festival would you attend? _ _ _ _ _ _ _ _
_ _ _ _ _ _ _ _ _ _ _ _   _ _ _ _ _ _ _ _

2. You are the biggest country music fan in the world! Which city hosts the festival that's definitely on your "to do" list?
_ _ _ _ _ _ _ _ _

3. You cook up the best-tasting pot of barbecue in Tennessee. You and your pig are headed to Henderson for the _ _ _ _ _ _ _
_ _ _ _ _ _   _ _ _ _ _ _   _ _ _ _ _ _ _ _ _
_ _ _ _ _ _ _ _ _!

4. Your grandma is a quilter who lives in Algood. You and your family are going to see the beautiful quilts she's entering in the
_ _ _ _ _   _ _ _ _ _ _ _ _ _ _   _ _ _ _ _
_ _ _ _ _ _ _ _.

**ANSWERS:** 1-National Storytelling Festival; 2-Nashville; 3-Chester County Annual Barbecue Festival; 4-Upper Cumberland Quilt Festival

# "T" Is For The Great State of Tennessee

**The words below are known as an *acrostic*. See if you can make up your own acrostic poem describing Tennessee. For each letter in Tennessee's name, write down a word or phrase that describes Tennessee. The first is done for you.**

T is for <u>the Three States of Tennessee</u>

E is for ______________________________

N is for ______________________________

N is for ______________________________

E is for ______________________________

S is for ______________________________

S is for ______________________________

E is for ______________________________

E is for ______________________________